The Earth Is the
LORD'S
•Christians and the Environment•

—————— Editors ——————
Richard D. Land & Louis A. Moore

BROADMAN PRESS
NASHVILLE, TENNESSEE

4216-27

ISBN: 0-8054-1627-7

Dewey Decimal Classification: 261.836

Subject Heading: CHRISTIANITY AND THE ENVIRONMENT

Library of Congress Card Catalog Number: 92-3769

Printed in the United States of America

Scripture quotations marked KJV are from the *King James Version of the Bible.*
Scripture quotations marked RSV are from the *Revised Standard Version of the Bible,* copyrighted 1946, 1952, © 1971, 1973.
Scripture quotations marked NIV are from the Holy Bible, *New International Version,* copyright © 1973, 1978, 1984 by International Bible Society.
Scripture quotations marked NASB are from the *New American Standard Bible.* © The Lockman Foundation, 1960, 1962, 1963, 1968, 1971, 1972, 1975, 1977. Used by permission.

Library of Congress Cataloging-in-Publication Data

The Earth Is the Lord's / edited by Richard D. Land and Louis A. Moore.

     p.   cm.

"This volume is the result of the twenty-fourth annual seminar of the Southern Baptist Convention Christian Life Commission, entitled 'Christians and the Environment,' held in Fort Worth, Texas, March, 1991"--Introd.

ISBN 0-8054-1627-7

1. Human ecology--Religious aspects--Christianity--Congresses. 2. Human ecology--Moral and ethical aspects--Congresses. I. Land, Richard D., 1946- . II. Moore, Louis, 1946-

    BT695.E27 1992
    261.8'362--dc20   *# 25282139*

                                   92-3769
                                       CIP

To the staff of the
Southern Baptist Christian Life Commission
and to our Board of Trustees

Preface

The psalmist said it well: "The earth is the Lord's, and the fulness thereof; the world, and they that dwell therein" (Ps. 24:1, KJV). Too often we humans, including we Christians, fail to emphasize God's ownership of all the world contains and of our responsibility to care for God's creation.

We compiled this book to stimulate Christian thinking about pressing needs in terms of caring for the environment.

The book originated in discussions surrounding the Southern Baptist Christian Life Commission's 24th annual seminar in Fort Worth, Texas, in March, 1991. It grew in the soil enriched by concern both at the Christian Life Commission and Broadman Press that Christians should be doing more in the area of ecology.

Special thanks goes to Edith Wilson, the CLC's editorial assistant, who painstakingly checked the manuscripts for accuracy, and to David S. Dockery for his guidance throughout the project.

We pray that God will use this book to help Christians to understand the width and breadth of their responsibility in caring for God's world, which He so wonderfully made and loaned to us.

Richard D. Land and Louis A. Moore, editors

July 31, 1991

Contents

IV

The Homiletic Challenge

V

The Practical Application

Contributors

Chapter 1. RICHARD D. LAND, Executive Director of the Southern Baptist Convention Christian Life Commission. He holds an A.B. degree from Princeton University, an M.Div. degree from New Orleans Baptist Theological Seminary, and a D.Phil. from Oxford University.

Chapter 2. MORRIS H. CHAPMAN, President and Treasurer of the SBC Executive Committee, former President of the Southern Baptist Convention, and former pastor of the 7,700-member First Baptist Church of Wichita Falls, Texas. He was President of the SBC Pastors' Conference in 1986. He received his B.A. degree from Mississippi College and his M.Div. and D.Min. degrees from Southwestern Baptist Theological Seminary.

Chapters 3 and 5. MILLARD ERICKSON, Research Professor of Theology at Southwestern Baptist Theological Seminary and former Vice President and Dean at Bethel Theological Seminary in St. Paul, Minnesota. He received his B.A. degree from the University of Minnesota, his B.D. degree from the Northern Baptist Theological Seminary, his M.A. degree from the University of Chicago, and his Ph.D. from Northwestern University.

Chapter 4. L. RUSS BUSH, III, Vice President for Academic Affairs and Dean of the Faculty at Southeastern Baptist Theological Seminary and a former professor of Philosophy of Religion at Southwestern Baptist Theological Seminary. He received his B.A. degree from Mississippi College and his M.Div. and Ph.D. degrees from Southwestern Baptist Theological Seminary.

Chapter 6. GARY H. LEAZER, director of the Interfaith Witness Department of the SBC Home Mission Board. He received his B.A. degree from Mississippi College and his M.Div. and Ph.D. degrees from Southwestern Baptist Theological Seminary.

Chapter 7. DAVID S. DOCKERY, Dean of the School of Theology and Associate Professor of Theology at Southern Baptist

Theological Seminary, former General Editor of Broadman Press, and a former professor at Criswell College. He received his B.S. degree from the University of Alabama, an M.A. from Texas Christian University, his M.Div. from Southwestern Baptist Theological Seminary, and his Ph.D. from the University of Texas at Arlington.

Chapter 8. WILLIAM M. PINSON, JR., Executive Director of the Executive Committee of the Baptist General Convention of Texas, a former professor at Southwestern Baptist Theological Seminary, and former President of Golden Gate Baptist Theological Seminary. He received his B.A. degree from North Texas State University, his B.D., M.Div., and his Ph.D. degrees from Southwestern Baptist Theological Seminary.

Chapter 9. JACK N. GRAHAM, pastor of Prestonwood Baptist Church in Dallas. Graham received his B.S. degree from Hardin-Simmons University and his M.Div. and D. Min. degrees from Southwestern Baptist Theological Seminary.

Chapter 10. ROBERT E. NAYLOR, President Emeritus of Southwestern Baptist Theological Seminary. He received his B.A. degree from East Central State Teachers College in Oklahoma and his Th.M. degree from Southwestern Baptist Theological Seminary.

Chapter 11. T. RICK IRVIN, Associate Professor of the Louisiana State University Institute for Environmental Studies and Research Director of the LSU Center for Energy Studies. He received his B.S. degree from the University of Georgia and his Ph.D. from the Massachusetts Institute of Technology.

Chapter 12. LOUIS A. MOORE, Director of Media and Products for the SBC Christian Life Commission and former Religion Editor of the *Houston Chronicle*. He received his B.A. degree from Baylor University and his M.Div. from Southern Baptist Theological Seminary.

Chapter 13. LAMAR E. COOPER, SR., Director of Denominational Relations for the SBC Christian Life Commission. He received his B.A. degree from Louisiana College and his Th.M and Ph.D. degrees from New Orleans Baptist Theological Seminary.

Introduction

Richard D. Land and Louis A. Moore

This volume originated from the 24th annual seminar of the Southern Baptist Convention Christian Life Commission, held in Fort Worth, Texas, in March 1991. The Christian Life Commission staff designed the seminar, entitled "Christians and the Environment: Finding a Biblical Balance Between Idolatry and Irresponsibility," as a major effort to initiate an ongoing discussion among Southern Baptists and other evangelicals about the environment and ecology.

We addressed such issues as: What does the Bible reveal about God's attitude toward His creation? What does God expect of human beings in relation to the care, stewardship, and development of the creation? What are our responsibilities and privileges as "earth-stewards" and "earth-keepers"?

Also, what are the theological and ethical implications of the biblical revelation about creation and the environment? Where do we agree and disagree with other environmental groups and why? How do we challenge Christians to become informed and involved on environmental issues? What are the practical applications of the environment and ecology issues in our workaday lives? What is the actual scientific situation at present? What can individuals, families, and churches *do* to make a difference? These are just some of the questions with which this volume and the seminar that precipitated it attempt to wrestle with and to answer.

The seminar's logo represented the approach from which the subject was addressed. The logo depicted the planet earth with the phrase "Divine Ownership" around the globe's top and the phrases "Human Stewardship" and "Personal Responsibility" occupying the rest of the planet's circumference. "Divine Ownership" acknowledged the Bible's declaration that "The earth is the

Lord's, and the fulness thereof" (Ps. 24:1, KJV). "Human Stewardship" referred to God's giving humankind "rule over the fish of the sea, and over the birds of the air, over the livestock, over all the earth, and over all the creatures that move along the ground" (Gen. 1:26, NIV). "Personal Responsibility" delineated each individual's responsibility to work and to take care of the creation (Gen. 2:15).

Within the context of God's ownership, corporate human stewardship obligations, and the personal responsibility of individuals, Christians must find the biblical balance or middle way between the idolatry that worships the "created things rather than the Creator" (Rom. 1:25, NIV) and the irresponsibility that assumes the right to treat God's creation as its own to do with as it pleases (Luke 12:13-21).

After the Christian Life Commission announced the seminar program, the agency received several letters of concern that scientists did not predominate among the speakers. One letter inquired: "Why just have a lot of theologians and preachers?" At the same time we received letters from scientists, including one who said, "I am so pleased someone is finally having a seminar on the environment with someone other than scientists as speakers." The scientists said we all needed to hear from the realm of religion and ethics on these issues. They were right. Scientists are critically important in diagnosing the problem technically and in prescribing scientific remedies, but they cannot answer the theological, moral, and ethical questions critical to the environmental debate. It is precisely at the point of theological and ethical perspective that we hope this present volume makes a genuine contribution.

The Environment: Urgent and Important

The present chapters have, in the process of being adapted from an oral presentation format, been edited and reorganized into subject groups, with some new material added. The first two chapters are introductory. Christian Life Commission Executive Director Richard D. Land begins by producing an "Overview" on "Beliefs and Behaviors." It attempts to introduce both the urgency and the importance of the environmental issue and to survey how the ecology debate has developed in the last quarter century.

Additionally, Morris Chapman, president and treasurer of the Southern Baptist Convention Executive Committee, addresses how important it is for Southern Baptists to follow Jesus' admonition to be salt and light and applies it to the ecology issue.

The next section falls under the subheading of *The Theological Imperative*. Millard J. Erickson, research professor of theology at Southwestern Baptist Theological Seminary, provides an in-depth prolegomenon to a theology of ecology. Erickson lays the biblical foundation for a positive, theologically mandatory response to biblical teaching on creation and environmental stewardship.

L. Russ Bush, academic dean of Southeastern Baptist Theological Seminary, Wake Forest, North Carolina, addresses a different, but important and timely question. Employing his academic training in the philosophy of religion, Bush provides a provocative analysis of humanistic and New Age ideas and how they to varying degrees permeate much of the secular, and even some religious aspects, of the modern environmentalist movement.

The next section, subheaded *Ethical Application*, consists of three chapters. The first chapter, once again by Millard Erickson, applies Christian ethical principles to the environment question and in so doing furnishes many important insights and points for discussion. The next chapter, by William M. Pinson, Jr., executive director of the Baptist General Convention of Texas and a former professor of ethics, speaks to the issue of "A Biblical Stewardship of God's Resources" from a denominational perspective. Pinson's persistent and searching application of the stewardship principle helps in dealing with the environment issue. The next chapter in this section, written by Gary H. Leazer, director of the Interfaith Witness Department of the Southern Baptist Home Mission Board, Atlanta, Georgia, analyzes the New Age movement and its environmental ethic and how it contrasts with biblical revelation at numerous critical points. The final chapter in this section, by David S. Dockery, dean of the School of Theology at Southern

Baptist Theological Seminary, brings together the issues related to the environment from the perspective of biblical ethics and exposition.

The next section, *The Homiletic Challenge*, helps those who want to develop in a local church a preaching program on matters related to creation and the environment. Baptists are people of the Word. They also are people of the spoken word through preaching. Individuals must use the pulpit to inform, challenge, and energize Southern Baptists on environmental issues. Included are two examples of applying the homiletic art to the task. The first is by Jack N. Graham, pastor of Prestonwood Baptist Church, Dallas, Texas, and the second is by Robert E. Naylor, president emeritus of Southwestern Baptist Theological Seminary.

The last section, *Practical Application*, begins with a provocative article by T. Rick Irvin, associate professor, Institute for Environmental Studies and research director, Center for Energy Studies, Louisiana State University, Baton Rouge, Louisiana. Professor Irvin gives a broad status report of the scope of industrial pollution and hazardous waste and their disastrous effects in the U.S. and around the world.

This is followed by a chapter by Louis A. Moore, director of media and product development of the Christian Life Commission, on how Christians can deal more constructively with the media on ecological issues and can make their desired points effectively. The last chapter, written by Lamar E. Cooper, also of the Christian Life Commission program staff, discusses the importance of recycling, details how a local church can begin a recycling program, and describes how such programs can help preserve God's creation.

I
Introductory

1
Overview:
Beliefs and Behaviors
Richard D. Land

We daily are more aware, especially in the industrialized world, that land, sea, and air pollution caused by human ignorance and irresponsibility is endangering Planet Earth. *Ecology* has been defined as "the study of the balance of living things in nature," but in recent decades people have expanded it also to encompass "the destruction man has brought upon nature."[1]

When Francis Schaeffer added that latter definition and commented on it 22 years ago in his book, *Pollution and the Death of Man: The Christian View of Ecology,* he was in a distinct minority among evangelical Christians in his sensitivity to environmental issues. Air pollution, toxic waste, tropical deforestation, depletion of the ozone layer, and the spate of local disputes over landfills have done much in the intervening two decades to focus our attention on the ecological crisis. More and more individuals now are aware that real, often critical, environmental problems exist, requiring serious, thoughtful responses. Both the problems and the concern they arouse have reached the stage in which something must and will be done in this, the last decade of the twentieth century.

Evangelical Christians must decide whether we will engage the issue and aggressively join the debate or whether we will continue to leave the field to a largely secular environmentalist movement which "sometimes sounds as though the creation of man was an act of aggression against the animal and mineral kingdoms," as

one commentator recently observed. The pantheistic and idolatrous tendencies exhibited by some elements of the environmentalist movement should concern Christians seriously.

In their efforts to create attitudes of value and worth for nature,
"some modern thinkers have called for worshiping the natural order and they speak of that order in terms of a unity and purpose
not allowing for an external creator," as Peter Hill pointed out in
his article, "Biblical Principles Applied to a Natural Resources/
Environment Policy."[2] Similarly, Schaeffer has observed:

> The term "God's creation" has no real place in pantheistic think-
> ing. One simply does not have a *creation*, but only an extension of
> God's essence in which any such term as "God's creation"—as
> though He were a personal God who created, whose creation was
> external to Himself (all of which is wrapped up in our Western
> phrase "God's creation")—has no place.[3]

In fact, all people, Christian and non-Christian, should be deeply concerned about such pantheistic thinking because it allows for
no really meaningful distinction between different aspects of creation, namely, human beings and other creatures. Consequently,
pantheistic thinking lowers human beings rather than elevating
the natural order. Whether the pantheistic thinking is "modern
scientism that related everything back to the energy particle, or
whether it is Eastern, and more religious and mystical in nature,
eventually nature does not become high but man becomes *low*."[4]

In the end, in the West, those who seek to argue for a special,
unique place of value for human beings in creation are accused of
anthropocentric, arrogant "speciesism"—defined as the artificial,
erroneous, egocentric valuing of one's own species more highly
than one ought. In Eastern pantheism (as in India), people allow
cows and rats to consume food needed by human beings. Animals
prosper while humans starve on the streets because no way exists
to make a meaningful value judgment between a human being and
a cow.

Many influential thinkers within the modern environmental

movement not only espouse such views and beliefs which are antithetical to Judeo-Christian values but also believe Christianity deserves substantial blame for Western culture's often callous disregard and flagrant exploitation of nature and of the environment.

Almost a quarter of a century ago, Lynn White, Jr., a history professor at UCLA, wrote an extremely influential article entitled "The Historical Roots of Our Ecologic Crisis"[5] published in *Science* magazine. White argued that while we live in a post-Christian world, we still operate under and "in a context of Christian axioms."[6]

White's thesis was that Christianity, at least "in its Western form, is the most anthropocentric religion the world has seen."[7] Believing that Christianity taught humanity's transcendence of, and domination of, nature as a God-given trait and right, White asserted that Christianity bore "a huge burden of guilt" for encouraging humanity's despoliation of nature.[8]

White then made two statements, which were extremely perspicacious and revealing. First, he said:

What people do about their ecology depends on what they think about themselves in relation to things around them. Human ecology is deeply conditioned by beliefs about our nature and destiny —that is, by religion. To Western eyes this is very evident in, say, India, or Ceylon. It is equally true of ourselves and of our medieval ancestors.[9]

He then reinforced the point, came back to it, and said:

What we do about ecology depends on our ideas of the man-nature relationship. More science and more technology are not going to get us out of the present ecologic crisis until we find a new religion, or rethink our old one. . . . Both our present science and our present technology are so tinctured with orthodox Christian arrogance toward nature that no solution for our ecologic crisis can be expected from them alone. Since the roots of our trouble are so largely religious, the remedy must also be essentially religious. . . . We must rethink and refeel our nature and destiny.[10]

Bearing Witness to the Creator

First, White is absolutely right in understanding the philosophical, religious, and ethical roots of the issue. As Francis Schaeffer concluded about this particular passage by White, "Men *do* what they *think*. Whatever their world view is, this is the thing which will spill over into the external world."[11]

What we think about who we are and what our relation is to the Creator and His creation absolutely determines how we deal with this issue, as well as how we deal with many others. The religious, the philosophical, and the ethical must be most important.

Second, White and others who blame Christianity for the world's ecological plight have stated repeatedly that they want to alter that Judeo-Christian world-view influence on our culture and even to alter the Judeo-Christian world view itself. Third, they have misunderstood and misinterpreted the Judeo-Christian revelation.

In part, they have misunderstood because Christians themselves have misunderstood and/or misapplied the message. Certainly, Christianity in its historical expressions has had its blind spots, even in its brightest moments, even in the midst of the Reformation epoch.[12]

Francis Schaeffer addressed this very point:

At certain points the people in the stream of the Reformation were inconsistent with the biblical teaching they claimed to follow. Many areas existed in which people did not follow the Bible as they should have, but two are outstanding: first, a twisted view of race, and second, a noncompassionate use of accumulated wealth.[13]

I believe we should add as a third area or category of a major blind spot a failure adequately to understand and/or bear witness to a truly biblical view of creation and humanity's relation to it and to the God who created them both. Far too often what its critics such as White have rejected is not true Christianity, not even Lewis' "mere Christianity," but a "sub-Christian" theory and/or practice in a post-Christian era.[14]

What then is truly a biblical view of the environment and humanity's relation to and responsibility for it? First, God reveals that He is the Creator (Gen. 1:1). That is a basic presupposition. Second, He reveals that His creation is valuable to Him, apart from humanity, by referring to other aspects of creation as "good" before He created human beings (Gen. 1:4, 10, 12, 18, 21, 25). Human beings don't appear until Genesis 1:26, and the term "good" has been used in verses 4, 10, 12, 18, 21, and 25. Third, this care for creation survives the Fall. In Genesis 9:8-17, NIV God tells Noah that He was establishing a covenant "with you" and "with every living creature." Then He speaks of "a covenant between me and the earth." And the sign of that covenant was the rainbow. We should not allow God's rainbow to be commandeered and prostituted by the New Age movement. It is a biblical and Christian symbol, and we ought to contend for it rather than to surrender it to our opponents.

Fourth, God's concern for and "valuing" of the creation has an eschatological dimension as well. God's redemption in Christ involves nature as well as humankind. The apostle Paul declared:

> The creation waits in eager expectation for the sons of God to be revealed. For the creation was subjected to frustration, not by its own choice, but by the will of the one who subjected it, in hope that the creation itself will be liberated from its bondage to decay and brought into the glorious freedom of the children of God (Rom. 8:19-21, NIV).

This does not mean that we will redeem the cosmos from the devastating effects of the Fall. It does mean that "cosmic regeneration" (*palingenesia*, [Matt. 19:28]) is part of Christ's ultimate redemption ministry.[15] The creation is important enough to God that God looks upon it as part of those things to be redeemed by the sacrifice, the death, the resurrection, the ascension and the second advent of our Lord and Savior Jesus Christ.

Fifth, God tells us that "The earth is the Lord's, and the fulness thereof" (Ps. 24:1, KJV). Yet, He also tells human beings that we are to have dominion (Hebrew *radah*, meaning "to rule") over the creation and to subdue it (Hebrew *kabash*, meaning "to bring into bondage," Gen. 1:26-28). These are strong, dominant words in the biblical text and leave no room for doubt that God has placed human beings first in creation. This human preeminence in the created order is extended when God tells Noah, "Everything that lives and moves will be food for you. Just as I gave you the green plants, I now give you everything" (Gen. 9:3, NIV). Thus, sixth, while God gives human beings authority for ruling and superintending nature, He remains the Lord of creation. He is the Lord of the earth. We merely are vicars and vice-regents.

Seventh, this strong teaching of human preeminence and dominion in the created order is balanced by God's announcement that He put human beings in the creation "to dress it and to keep it" (Gen. 2:15, KJV). The verb "dress" (*avadh*) means "to work, to till" and keep (*shamar*) means "to keep, guard, protect." Other passages detail God's expectations that human beings carefully manage land (Lev. 25:1-5), wildlife (Deut. 22:6), and domestic animals (Deut. 25:4).

These passages tell us that creation belongs to God. As stewards of His property, we are responsible for protecting His creation. We come first. We must remember, however, that while human life demands reverence, all life deserves respect. We have the right to use animals and plants for human good. We do not have the right to disregard living things or to treat them as inanimate objects. We have the right to domesticate and to raise cattle and to use them for human food. We do not have the right to act in a callous, cruel, or cavalier manner toward any living creature. We have a right as painlessly as possible to use animals in research to better human health. I don't believe we have the right to use animals or to cause them discomfort merely to improve cosmetics.

These Scriptures also tell us that as stewards of His property, we are responsible to develop, but not to desecrate or dissipate, God's creation. We are required to develop God's creation and to bring forth its fruit and increase. Our Lord's Parable of the Talents

(Matt. 25:14-30) underscores the Genesis admonition to "dress" the garden. There, the servant who buried his talent was severely castigated for his poor stewardship and lack of productivity with the talent entrusted to his care (Matt. 25:24-29).

Perpetuating the Created Order

We should make one additional point. If we believe that God is the Creator and that He has created everything for a purpose, then that in itself has enormous significance and implications for the environmental issue. It is for the Christian an act of faith and an act of stewardship, as well as an act of enlightened self-interest, to seek the perpetuation and viability of all the created order until we can discern and discover what purpose God has for every living creature and plant.

A classic example is Madagascar's rosy periwinkle, which has been proven to have significant cancer-fighting properties. This benefit would have been lost to humankind if the plant had been eradicated before its anti-cancer potential had been discovered.

I am more firmly convinced than ever that we face an ecological crisis and that God holds us accountable for our stewardship of the creation and of its resources He has entrusted to our care. That, of course, includes our children. I believe we have a responsibility to inform our young people of the problems and of the biblical principles that should inform our response. In doing so, we can further perform our duties as Christians and parents by inoculating our young people against the false, anti-biblical teaching which so heavily suffuses so much of the modern, secular environmentalist movement.

If we don't tell our young people and tell Christians what we believe and why we believe it on this issue, who will? If we do not practice what we preach, many of our young people, who are deeply concerned about this issue, will be carried to places that we would rather they not go and will draw conclusions that we would rather they not draw by exposure to false philosophies. These philosophies, for fallacious and anti-biblical reasons, at least demonstrate concern about the creation.

We must help our young people and others by moving from ascertaining orthodoxy to advocating orthopraxy. We must move from principle to practice and from advice to application.

For those outside the Christian faith who have been environmentally involved, I have good news and bad news. The *good* news is that we repent of past insensitivity and neglect. The *bad* news is that

> There is...a distinctively Christian response to ecological concerns. The Christian doctrine of creation approaches the study from a different perspective, reaches conclusions from different assumptions, proposes solutions from those different assumptions and works at ecology for different reasons.[16]

We sometimes will agree with the secular environmentalists. We will often disagree, however, because we have a different approach and a different attitude. Consequently, these will require different actions. I pray that we will "be prepared to give an answer to everyone who asks you to give the reason" both as to why we do what we do and "for the hope" that we have by the providence and grace of God (1 Pet. 3:15, NIV).

Notes

1. Francis Schaeffer, *The Complete Works of Francis A. Schaeffer. A Christian World View* (6 vols.; Westchester, IL:Crossway, 1982), 5:4 from *Pollution and the Death of Man. The Christian View of Ecology* (1970).

2. Peter J. Hill, "Biblical Principles Applied to a Natural Resources/Environment Policy" *Christians in the Marketplace Series*, Vol. IV, *Biblical Principles and Public Policy* ed. Richard C. Chewning (Colorado Springs: NavPress, 1990), 170. There are four volumes in this very helpful series, partially sponsored by the business school at Baylor University, that deal from an evangelical perspective with the questions of the Christian in business and in the economic marketplace. This particular article deals with natural resources and environmental policy.

3. Schaeffer, *Complete Works*, 5:14-15.

4. Ibid. 5:18-19, emphasis supplied.

5. Reprinted as an Appendix to Schaeffer's *Pollution and the Death of Man* (1970) in Schaeffer, *Works*, 5:57-69. Cf. also Richard L. Means, "Why Worry About Nature?" *Saturday Review*, Dec. 2, 1967.

6. White, "The Historical Roots of our Ecological Crisis," in Schaeffer, *Works,* 5:63.

7. White in Schaeffer, *Works,* 5:64.

8. Ibid., 66.

9. Ibid., 63.

10. Ibid., 67-69.

11. Schaeffer, *Works,* 5:6.

12. Ibid., 123, 135, from *How Should We Then Live?* (1976).

13. Ibid., 5:141.

14. Ibid., 5:143-144.

15. *Criswell Study Bible,* ed. W. A. Criswell (Nashville: Thomas Nelson, 1979), 1139n.

16. William H. Stephens, *Doctrine of Creation* (Nashville: BSSB, 1990), Audio Cassette Resource.

2

Salt and Light in Our World
Morris H. Chapman

As we focus our attention on a Christian response to the environmental crisis, we first should look at Luke 12:48, KJV: "For unto whomsoever much is given, of him shall be much required." Let us also pay attention to the words of Jesus in Matthew 5:13-15, NIV:

> You are the salt of the earth. But if the salt loses its saltiness, how can it be made salty again? It is no longer good for anything, except to be thrown out, and trampled by men. You are the light of the world. A city on an hill cannot be hidden. Neither do people light a lamp and put it under a bowl. Instead they put it on its stand, and it gives light to everyone in the house.

Christians must obey the Lord's assignment to be the "salt" of the earth and the "light" of the world. Salt is a preservative—it stops decay. Salt is a disinfectant—it purifies and cleanses. Salt is a life-sustaining agent. Without it, living things perish. As born-again Christians, we must function in an infectious, decaying world as salt—preserving, disinfecting, and life-sustaining.

The Lord also commands us to be the light of the world. If salt is "defensive" then light is "offensive," punching holes in the darkness of ignorance, confusion, and blindness. As "light," we must illuminate the darkness, dispel the gloom, inform ignorance, and bring order from confusion. We should expand our understanding and learn new dimensions of the imperative to be salt and light as it relates to the environment.

We face major challenges. Pollution resulting from fossil fuel emissions, industrial waste, and human irresponsibility confronts us. Rapidly diminishing world resources confront us. Experts increasingly tell us we have no more than a decade left to reverse these alarming and destructive trends before we damage beyond repair our whole creation's infrastructure.

What must we do? How do we "preserve" as salt? How do we "illuminate" as light? I am deeply indebted to Richard Land of the Christian Life Commission for stimulating my thoughts as to how this can be done.

The problem is becoming more prominent in the minds of all Americans, and world citizens, for that matter. Consider this article from *The Washington Post*, which helps us not only to sense the ecological damage being done in the world today but also to consider the long-term effects of it.

Nearly two years after the grounded tanker *Exxon Valdez* dumped 10.9 million gallons of crude oil into Alaska's Prince William Sound, scientific studies have found new evidence of long-term damage to certain varieties of sea birds, salmon, trout, and other marine life. Although in some respects the Sound has proved surprisingly resilient, the available body of scientific evidence, including confidential, governmental documents obtained by *The Washington Post*, challenges the increasing, widespread assumption that the oil spill was a transitory event whose worst effects were cosmetic. Federal scientists have concluded, for example, that some colonies of the diving birds of the North Pacific, murres, have suffered a total failure to reproduce as a consequence of the spill, amounting to a loss of several hundred thousand chicks, according to sources. Federal scientists estimate that some sea bird colonies may require up to 70 years to recover. Another study suggests that oil may have reduced the populations of rock fish, herring, shrimp, mussels, and clams, among other marine organisms, presenting a considerable risk that some of the species may not respond to conventional management action for decades.[1]

The scorching flames and the billowing black smoke from the

oil fields of Kuwait painted a horrid picture of ecological destruction. The health of the Kuwaitis was at stake, and the pollution may be a hazard which long outlasts the destruction of buildings.

A Christian's Responsibility

What must we do? Some things we cannot control, but we can do things as salt and light, as Christians in a world God has created and over which He gave us dominion. In sin we lost much of that dominion, but we have not lost our responsibility in the world.

This book focuses on the dilemma Christians face as they seek to understand their biblical responsibility. We are responsible for thinking and acting biblically in relation to God's creation. In doing so, we must avoid the pantheistic extreme of idolizing the creation rather than the Creator. We also must avoid the unbiblical extreme of acting irresponsibly, assuming that we are free to treat God's creation as if it were ours to do with as we please.

God's Word repeatedly underscores the theme of God's ownership of creation. Psalm 24:1, KJV tells us "The earth is the Lord's, and the fulness thereof; the world, and they that dwell therein." Psalm 50:10-12, KJV declares "For every beast of the forest is mine, and the cattle upon a thousand hills. I know all the fowls of the mountains: and the wild beasts of the field are mine. . . . the world is mine, and the fulness thereof."

During the Persian Gulf War, I felt sad as I watched on television the struggling birds coated with the oil in the Gulf. Every Christian's heart must understand and be sensitive to the struggle for life. My heart ached as I watched these birds, because the life of this world is the only life these creatures will know. We must be sensitive to protection for those who cannot protect themselves. We also must be sensitive to productivity as we fulfill the responsibility God gives us on this earth as we wait for the coming of the Lord Jesus.

The truth that "the earth is the Lord's" raises for us the necessary concern of stewardship. The biblical concept of stewardship is essential in understanding how we are to be salt and light on the issue of the environment. The dictionary defines a steward as "One who manages another's property, finances, or other affairs; an administrator; supervisor."[2]

The New Testament clearly pictures this concept of the steward and stewardship. The steward is entrusted with the property of another. A brief look at the typical well-to-do household in New Testament times is both instructive and illustrative in understanding stewardship. In such a house (*oikos*) was a householder (*oiko-despotes*), the owner or "the goodman of the house" (Mark 14:14, KJV). In addition to the household (*oikeioi*), which included the family, also was the steward (*oikonomos*). The word *steward* is derived from two Greek words, *oikos*, meaning *house* and *nemo*, meaning *dispense* or *manage*. Thus, we get our word economics (*oikonomia*) from the Greek word for steward.

Jesus often used this commonly known household occupation in His parables. The steward is a prominent character in the Parable of the Wicked Husbandman (Matt. 21:33-46), the Parable of the Talents (Matt. 25:14-30), and the Parable of the Pounds (Luke 19:12-27).

He also used it in Luke 12:41-48 in the Parable of the Faithful and Unfaithful Servants, which concludes with the warning, "For unto whomsoever much is given, of him shall be much required" (Luke 12:48, KJV).

Also, the apostle Paul reminded the Corinthian church that "it is required in stewards, that a man be found faithful" (1 Cor. 4:2, KJV). We are stewards of God's creation, and we are responsible and accountable for our stewardship of what He has entrusted to our watchcare.

A Blessed Nation and People

The statement that "unto whomsover much is given, of him shall be much required" (Luke 12:48, KJV) is particularly relevant to us both as Americans and as Christians. We are blessed as a nation and as a people. God's providence has placed us in one of the most choice sections of God's vineyard. God has blessed our land beyond all measure in beauty and natural resources. In 1893

Katherine Lee Bates put into the eloquent song, *America the Beautiful*, what we all have observed and experienced:

> O beautiful for spacious skies,
> For amber waves of grain,
> For purple mountain majesties
> Above the fruited plain!
> America! America!
> God shed His grace on thee,
> And crown thy good with brotherhood,
> From sea to shining sea.

Most of us take such precious little time to thank God for the trees that grow and for the birds that sing. One Sunday my preschool director thrust a book into my hands and asked me to visit all classrooms in which we teach three-year-olds and to read the book to the children. In that book I read very simple statements about trees and birds and God's ownership—statements simple enough for children to understand. If children can understand this concept, so can adults. I challenge all Christians and all Americans and every world citizen to stop long enough to remember that our world exists because of our Father in heaven.

By God's providence we are blessed to be citizens of this great and glorious land. We have been doubly blessed to be named among the people of God. Few, if any, people in the history of Christendom have been more blessed with opportunities to sit under godly, biblical preaching and teaching of God's Word than are contemporary Christians in North America. "Unto whomsoever much is given, of him shall much be required."

I want to share three important issues with you: how privileged we are, how pressing is the task, and how personal is the responsibility.

First, we indeed are privileged. Those great privileges and blessings bring monumental responsibilities. We have been entrusted with much, and we are responsible for how we use, or abuse, these blessings. How in a generation as a people who batter and abuse one another shall we learn the privilege of caring for the fowl of the air?

As our Lord's teachings indicate, we are accountable for using what God has entrusted to us responsibly and productively. The language of Luke 12:48 is the language of business, indicating capital invested with an expectation that it will not be squandered or merely lie idle but will be improved and increased. This idea is employed as well in the Parable of the Pounds (Luke 19:20-24) and the Parable of the Talents (Matt. 25:24-30). In relation to the environment, it will not be sufficient merely to preserve but also to produce from what God has entrusted to our care.

Second, the task before us is a pressing one. Decay and degeneration in a fallen world is constant. The need to care for, and tend to, God's creation so that it may be preserved and productive is incessant. As humanity's capacity to pollute and destroy increases geometrically with the expansion of industrialization, the responsibility is more urgent. Also, as Jesus reminds the disciples in Luke 12:41-48, the Lord may well "come on a day when he does not expect him and at an hour he is not aware of" (Luke 12:46, NIV). Ultimately, this will be fulfilled in an eschatological sense, and for those whose death precedes our Lord's return, the time for rectifying lassitude, idleness, and irresponsibility will pass suddenly and unexpectedly.

Third, please notice how personal is our responsiblity. Each person is responsible and accountable for his or her actions. It is imperative that we think through what we have and where we are going on this earth.

As the apostle Paul reminded the Christians in Rome, "each one of us will give an account of himself to God" (Rom. 14:12, NIV). God holds each of us accountable for the proper stewardship of the blessings, talents, and worldly goods He entrusts to our care. This emphatically includes natural resources and the environment. God is concerned about His creation. He has given us duties and responsibilities as stewards "to work it and take care of it" (Gen. 2:15, NIV), meaning to protect it and develop it. And "it is required in stewards" that they "be found faithful" (1 Cor. 4:2, KJV).

We clearly are obliged to be salt and light on the environmental and ecological issues of the day. We have a pressing duty to be informed and involved. We have increased responsibility because God has blessed us as a country and as a denomination. And we will give a personal account of our stewardship of His earth and His resources. The two questions of the hour are: Have we been protective, and have we been productive?

"From the one who has been entrusted with much, much more will be required."

Notes

1. *The Washington Post*, February 21, 1991, A-7. ©1991, *The Washington Post*. Reprinted with permission.

2. William Morris, ed., *The American Heritage Dictionary of the English Language* (Boston: Houghton Mifflin & Co.), 1254.

II
The Theological Imperative

3
Biblical Theology of Ecology
Millard J. Erickson

When we discuss concern about the world and the entire environment, we first must try to ascertain what God says about it, about us, and about the relationship among these three factors. As Christians, we have a special stake in establishing clearly the biblical teachings bearing upon the ecological concern.

Several reasons exist for establishing this special stake, but we focus here on one in particular. Our world has an ecological crisis, whether or not we realize and acknowledge it. One frequently hears charges that Christianity, and especially conservative or evangelical Christianity, is the major culprit in this crisis. This is deemed true both because of Christians' behavior and also because Christianity's ideology justifies or even implies such behavior. Therefore, people feel that Christians merely are carrying out the logical implications of their belief system.[1]

Actually, the indictment is not a single charge but a whole series of them. We note four in particular:

1. The call to have dominion over the earth, in Genesis 1:28, entails treating the earth as being important only to support the good of the human being. This therefore leads to exploitation and rape of the earth.[2]

2. Christianity has condoned modern science and technology's exploitation of the earth.[3]

3. Christianity has promoted a dualism, according to which the natural or the physical or the secular is of less value, or even is

negative in character, compared with the spiritual or the otherworldly.[4]

4. Belief in the second coming, which will usher in Christ's complete and perfect reign, effectively removes any reason for us to be concerned about ecology.[5]

In light of these charges, some people contend that for ecological reasons, Eastern religions, with their pantheistically based appreciation and virtual reverence for nature, must supplant Christianity.[6]

Major Biblical Themes

The Christian has two reasons for investigating the biblical teachings bearing upon nature and ecology. The first is evangelistic in nature. If Christianity is to positively influence a world increasingly concerned about ecological issues and if it is to win and retain the commitment of concerned, sensitive persons, it must demonstrate that its ideology does not contribute to the ecological crisis. Beyond that, however, as a matter of discipleship, it must ascertain the true teachings of Scripture on these matters, so that its practice correctly may fulfill God's intention for us.

This chapter's aim, then, is to to draw out and in some sense synthesize or systematize major biblical and theological themes. These themes are as follows:

1. In the biblical understanding of things, God has created everything. As well known and widely accepted as this is in Christian circles, it nonetheless needs to be documented and elucidated. This doctrine is an important backdrop for all aspects of Christian understanding because it stands at the very opening of the Bible: "In the beginning, God created the heaven and the earth" (Gen. 1:1, KJV). The expression, "the heaven and the earth," which simply is a Hebrew idiom for "all that exists," portrays the inclusiveness of this action.

This doctrine occurs other places as well. It even occurs in the New Testament, where the Bible attributes creative activity to the Word, Christ Himself. John 1:3, NIV says, "Through him all things were made; without him nothing was made that has been made." Paul clearly says twice in Colossians 1:16, NIV "by him all things were created." It is apparent that to the Scripture writers the universe and all within it was not simply something that was there; it had come from God and owed its existence to Him. It is the creation, for it has been created.

This understanding also permeates the religious practice of the Hebrew believers, especially as expressed in the Psalms (for example, Psalm 19). Here the writer glorifies, praises, and thanks God because He has brought the entire universe into being. The worshiper especially acknowledges God's greatness in creating and watching over the universe. The worshiper also gives God credit and thanks for his own existence.

We also must note the variety and complexity of God's creating work. He made many different kinds of creatures, each on its own day, and each *after its kind*. Each was a creation of God, and evidently each was an important part of His creating work. It was only when He completed the entire process that God looked upon His creation and pronounced it *very good*.

Nor was this the end of God's originating work. If we believe, as the Bible teaches, that God is in control of all that happens in His creation, causing it to fulfill His intended purposes, then its continued growth of variety and complexity also is God's work, even if He does not do this directly. It is part of the ongoing work of the Holy Spirit making the entire creation fruitful (Isa. 32:15). Thus it is good that the creation has this fullness and richness.[7] So each part of the creation, each type, each "kind" in the biblical terminology, is important in making the creation all that it is. Eliminating any one of these kinds consequently is a loss that God regrets.

On a continuing basis, numerous species are becoming extinct. It may seem a small matter to us when some obscure species, such as the snail darter, of which numerous similar species exist, passes out of existence. Yet in God's sight, the creation has, at least to some degree, become a bit impoverished as a result.

The flood account additionally indicates this same principle. There God commanded Noah to take seven of every kind of clean animal, a male and its mate, and two of every kind of unclean animal, a male and its mate, as well as every kind of bird, male and female (Gen. 7:2-3). The reason given was, "to keep their various kinds alive throughout the earth" (v. 3, NIV). It evidently was important that all of the creation He had brought into being be preserved, rather than part of it being lost.

Beyond this, however, the Bible depicts God as still the owner of all this, since He gave everything existence, which it otherwise would not have had. While He has lent or entrusted these resources to His creatures to watch over, develop, and maximize, it is a case of *lending* it, not *giving* it. He is still the rightful owner.

This is another way of saying that He is truly the *Lord* of all of creation. The creation is to obey Him and to carry out His will. This, however, occurs in different ways by different types of creatures. The physical creation obeys Him *mechanically*. It functions according to natural laws with which it has been structured. The animals obey God *instinctively*. Their actions manifest impulses God divinely implanted within them. Humans, however, have the capacity to obey God *voluntarily*. They can choose to obey or disobey.

Each of these types of creatures glorifies God by obeying Him. That obedience shows the greatness and wisdom of God, His superiority over all that is. The degree of glory increases with the elevation in the scale, so that the human brings greater glory to the Maker by honoring Him than do the rock or the plant. Yet what the psalmist wrote still is true: "The heavens declare the glory of God" (Ps. 19:1, KJV).

God's Love for Creation

We must remember, however, that the creation's ability to carry out His divine purpose depends to a large extent on whether it is in the state of perfection in which He created it. To whatever degree it has lost something of that pristine purity He gave it, it will imperfectly manifest that power, wisdom, and splendor characteristic of its Maker.[8]

We have some indications that the creation is not all that it was intended to be, that it is in some sense "fallen." Paul, in a difficult passage, Romans 8:18-25, speaks of the creation as being in bondage. It appears, from v. 20, that this is in some sense tied to the sin of humans. Two possible meanings seem to exist for this. Both of them probably bear upon the matter at hand.

The first is that because of the human sin, God pronounced a curse. In that curse, God affected the creation in certain ways which keep it from witnessing to God's glory and greatness as God originally intended. Thus, the farmer encountering thorns and thistles as he works, and the toilsome, burdensome character of work, as well as the mother giving birth in anguish, are experiencing the effects of the Fall. They do not necessarily experience the creation as "very good" and thus as the product of the good Creator.

A second possible meaning of Paul's statement is that humans, through their sinful activity, bring the creation into bondage. Nature frequently is the victim of people's greed and selfishness, as people seek to obtain the maximum of material good at minimal cost. Plundering and polluting the environment, however, enslaves and binds it, affecting its ability to bear adequate witness to its Maker.

We can do relatively little to alter the first matter we mentioned, since the effect largely was one time, major and permanent, although medicine, agriculture and technology have helped at some points. However, since the latter group of effects represents things we inflict on the creation more directly, we have both a responsibility and an opportunity to be stewards of preserving and optimizing the creation.

2. According to the biblical teaching, God loves and considers valuable every part of the creation. We know well the many statements about God's love for humans. One of the best known of these is Jesus' statement in Matthew 10:29-30, comparing the Father's care for humans with His watch over and protection of birds of the air. He notes that not even a sparrow, trivial though its value may be, can fall to the earth without the Father's knowledge

and permission. The passage's main emphasis is, of course, that God loves and cares for human beings, but the argument's logic depends on the fact of God's love and care for other creatures. The argument is something like this:

Because of their value to Him, God watches over birds of the air. You are more valuable to God than many sparrows. Therefore, God will watch over you to an even greater extent.

While not explicit, this seems to be the underlying structure of the argument. If this is the case, then the first premise must be true in order for the conclusion to follow as true.

Another interesting passage occurs in the Old Testament at the very end of the Book of Jonah. God had called Jonah to preach in Nineveh, but he had refused. God then used some persuasion to overcome this reluctance, so that Jonah went to Nineveh, preached the message of impending divine judgment, the people repented, and judgment was averted. Instead of being pleased, however, Jonah was unhappy that God had not destroyed the city. God replied, "But Nineveh has more than a hundred and twenty thousand people who cannot tell their right hand from their left, and many cattle as well. Should I not be concerned about that great city?" (Jonah 4:11, NIV) *And also many cattle!* the Book of Jonah offered that amazing statement as a partial explanation for God's not destroying the city. Apparently, God's reluctance to destroy the many cattle was a factor in His forbearance. Those animals were of value to Him; He did not want their lives lost.

Living Responsibly with God's Gift

We must keep in mind a proper balance between God's transcendence and His immanence. Where the transcendence is emphasized excessively, His involvement with and care and concern for His creation is overlooked.[9] On the contrary, however, Scripture pictures God as intimately involved with the creation. As Odil Steck writes, "The one God Yahweh is now, as creator, related to the whole of the natural world in general and to everything that lives in it."[10]

3. God has, at least *in part*, provided the rest of creation for the human race's use and enjoyment.[11] In Genesis 1:29, God told Adam that He had provided food for him with every seed-bearing plant and every tree that has fruit with seed in it. He also gave these plants to the animals for food. Then, in Genesis 9:3, after the flood, God gave people for food every moving animal as well. Although not the sole reason that these various creatures existed, they existed at least in part then and exist now to sustain and nurture the human. Nothing is wrong, therefore, when humans utilize the rest of the creation to sustain their own lives and to meet their legitimate needs. They must, of course, be certain they do this in a way which does not violate or compromise any other of God's commands or principles.

Note, however, to whom God gave the whole creation. It was to *Adam*, both a proper noun or name and a common noun. Adam was a definite historical individual. Let us make no mistake about that. He is not simply or merely a symbol of the human race. Nevertheless, he and Eve were the entire human race at that point. Adam contained within him, germinally or seminally, all humans who ever will be within the span of history. God did not promise and provide to Adam alone the rest of creation as a benefit for humans. God did not intend for Adam alone to enjoy its benefits. God intended for these benefits to accrue to all members of the human race, at all times.

How do we know this promise was to Adam, humankind, rather than to Adam, the individual? We see evidence for this more generalized or universalized understanding in the fact that God repeated this promise and even broadened it to Noah after the Fall. Indeed, the very way God states this is significant. God says, "Just as I gave you the green plants, I now give you everything" (Gen. 9:3, NIV). The Bible does not tell us of any such statement to Noah. When God gave the green plants to Adam, it meant He had given them to Noah, as Adam's descendant.

Also, the continuing context indicates a universalized setting. For when God promised He never again would send a flood that would wipe out all life as this one had, He told Noah and his sons, "I now establish my covenant with you and with your descendants after you" (v. 9, NIV). When He gave the sign—the rainbow of the covenant—He indicated that the covenant was "for all generations to come" (v. 12, NIV). This indicated that God's entire covenantal commitment was not merely to a single generation but was to all generations that would ever exist.

We find in the scope of the Noahic covenant yet another evidence of God's care for the nonhuman creation. When God covenanted with Noah and his sons that He never again would send a flood to destroy all life on earth, He made this not merely with those humans but also with the entire "supporting cast," as it were: "I now establish my covenant with you and with your descendants after you and with every living creature that was with you—the birds, the livestock and all wild animals, all those that came out of the ark with you—every living creature on earth" (Gen. 9:9-10, NIV). The ensuing verses repeat five more times this same dimension of the covenant: "every living creature" (v. 12); "the earth" (v. 13); "all living creatures of every kind" (v. 15); "all living creatures of every kind on the earth" (v. 16); "all life on the earth" (v. 17). These are only statements explicitly about the covenant. These are in addition to the statements about not destroying all life. The intent of God, and the extent of His covenant, seems to be quite clear in this passage.[12]

We should note, however, that these statements as found in the Bible appear to apply only to living creatures; i.e., animals. The way God refers to them (e.g., "all those that came out of the ark with you" v. 10), seems quite definitely to refer to the animals. Does this mean that God's covenant and concern do not extend to the plants and the inanimate members of the creation?

We must observe that, in this context, God envisioned destruction by flood and thus He promised such destruction would be avoided. Note, however, He makes no mention of destroying plants by the flood. Presumably, although the flood would destroy many of them, the various kinds survived this destruction of the then-existing individual members because the seeds would germinate, grow and provide new members. In some cases, the flood may not have been of sufficiently great duration to kill the plants involved. Note, for example, how the dove Noah sent forth returned with a freshly plucked leaf in its beak (Gen. 8:11). Also, such an event presumably could not destroy the physical universe, although such problems as erosion could occur.

We may conclude God's limiting the reference to the animals does not indicate He lacked concern for the other members of the creation, for they would not be subject to obliteration through drowning in a flood. Thus, the omission is not significant. We may not argue from silence in this case. Note, however, that we also are not given any positive evidence here of God's love for the rest of creation. Such a contention will have to come from another source.

We may observe, however, one other consideration bearing upon this issue. Although no direct evidence exists that the rest of creation is important and valuable to God and that He loved it, we may well have indirect or instrumental evidence of that. By this we mean that even if plants and minerals were not valuable in and of themselves, they are important to the extent they are necessary or at least contribute to the existence, survival and welfare of humans and of animals.

Whether we can identify it as love or not, we see definite indications of divine pleasure with the creation below animals. Thus, at the end of the third day, after He gathered the waters and the land and created plants, and at the end of the fourth day, after He made the sun and the moon, God said that it was good. This expression is identical to what God says at the end of the fifth day and on the sixth day, before He created the human. It is only when humans are introduced that it says He saw that it was "very good" (v. 31). In its context, however, the statement refers to God seeing *all* that He had made. Thus, it appears that the completeness of the creation is what stimulated God's extra pleasure. The judgment He forms here appears at least to be valuational—that it was good.

4. As we move from discussing the theological teachings regarding the creation to those dealing with aspects of the human relating especially to responsibility for this creation, one transitional point links these two areas. This is the fact that the human also is a part of the created world. Therefore, humans and the rest of creation are linked.

We note that the Bible lists the creation of the human being in the same passage with the creation of the other beings. One thing is distinct about the account—it says God created the other creatures "after their kind," whereas God made the human in His own image. Further, a second account elaborates upon how the human was fashioned (2:4-25). Thus, some points of similarity as well as points of difference evidently occur between the human and the other creatures. Interestingly, the creation of the human does not even involve a separate day of creation but occurs on the sixth day—the same day as the animals.

This means that in some sense we are kin with the rest of the creation. One does not have to hold that we are evolved from them to believe this. It merely means that, like them, we also are creatures and the same Creator has created us. Thus, like them, we are finite and depend on God for our existence. It also means that we share with them part of our purpose in life, namely, to obey and glorify God. If we fully realize this, we know that the empathy we feel or should feel for the other human beings also will, to a lesser extent, extend to the rest of the creation as well.

Interconnected with Others

The physical reality of this spiritual truth is that we are made of the same "ingredients," as it were, as are the other parts of the creation. Chemically, our bodies are made up of the same elements as are those of the animals, or the physical structure of the plants, the inanimate members of the universe, etc.

We need here to be aware of what I would call "anthropological docetism." We all are familiar with Christological docetism, which holds that Jesus' humanity was not genuine but only was apparent humanity, or partial humanity. This implies that Jesus does not (and cannot) really participate fully in the human race and therefore is not completely able to represent it, and thus, to redeem it by His death. The parallel is anthropological docetism, a situation in which humans are not thought of as participating fully in the realm of nature, as not really part of it. The separation between humanity and the rest of the creation is great and perhaps even qualitative in character. If such, we might tend to forget the limitations of our created nature and similarly neglect the interdependence of the human and the rest of the creation.

The general revelation also supports what we have sought to elucidate here from Scripture. The same natural laws governing the rest of the creation govern human beings as well. We most easily notice this with regard to those creatures closest to humans: the higher animals. The same conditions leading to the death of a mammal also will result in the death of a human.

5. We also need to amplify a further point. The various parts of the creation are interconnected and thus have an interdependency with and upon one another. We see this, for example, in the creation account in which God gives the plants for food, not only to the human but also to the other animals (Gen. 1:30). Then, later, God gave the animals to people for their consumption (Gen. 9:3). The lesson, by way of inference, is quite clear: The human ultimately depends, either directly or indirectly, upon the welfare of the plants. What is good for them also is good for the human.

This is empirically confirmed in a number of ways. Most of these ways, unfortunately, have been negative in their impact. The type of consumption requiring maximum productivity results in pollution of the atmosphere, which is forming an envelope of pollution around the earth, holding in the heat, while causing reflection of the sunlight back to earth. This appears to be resulting in global warming, so that discernible increases in the earth's temperature are one result. This in turn gradually results in melting the polar ice caps. This either will produce flooding of coastal cities such as Los Angeles, necessitating evacuation of low-lying areas, or will require building massive sea walls. Both of these exact great costs.

A more concrete example can be found in one of the central African republics, in which the numbers of hippopotamuses had been increasing to the point where they were becoming a considerable nuisance, as well as being unattractive, of course. The government modified the law to permit and even to encourage people to hunt these great creatures. This was done, but soon an outbreak of schistosomiasis occurred. Officials then discovered that a snail which lives in rivers spread the disease. When the hippopotamus population was reduced, the snail population multiplied unrestrained, with the consequent virtual epidemic of schistosomiasis.

These two cases illustrate the observation that when humans attempt, out of the best of motivations, to alter the balance of nature, they frequently end up upsetting the system, with unanticipated results. These results often are unfortunate for human beings. The fortunes of one part of the universe are tied up with those of other parts. It is appropriate that ecology bears that name, for it derives from the word *oikos*, meaning house. The creation is a household, in which occurrences in one part of the system affect other parts of it.

Perhaps nowhere is this common derivation of the human and the rest of creation seen more clearly than in the second creation account. There God is said to have taken "dust of the earth" and by breathing into it the breath of life made the human from it. We are not told precisely what this dust of the earth was. It may have been literal dust or earth, or it may have been some more basic raw material of all of reality such as matter or hydrocarbon molecules. However, this was not some already living being, since it is at this point that the human becomes a "living being," the same terminology used in Genesis 1:20, 21, 24, 28. Whatever the exact designation of this term, it appears to represent the common "stuff" of reality, tying the human closely into the rest of creation and combatting any tendency toward "anthropological docetism." In this sense, it fulfills a role similar to the one the birth narratives perform for Christology.

6. A most significant motif regarding the human, from our perspective, is that God has commissioned humans to be *stewards* of the created universe. That is to say, we are to rule over, tend, and maximize the creation. This is conveyed in several passages. A foundational one is Genesis 1:26-28, where God first purposed and then acted to create humankind in His own image and then gave people dominion over the rest of the creation. We first see this being implemented when Adam named the various animals (Gen. 2:19-20). We also see this in the flood account, where Noah brings the various animals into the ark. We see it both in those who till the ground and those who herd animals.

Note, however, that this management of the creation is not simply the same as saying that the creation exists for people's benefit and use. For this dominion is to be understood in light of God's role in relationship to the world and of the kings of Israel relative to the nation. It was a dominion, not for the sake of the one having dominion, but for the sake of the one or ones being ruled over. Thus, the kings of Israel were expected to show this type of concern for the people over whom they ruled.[13]

This means that animals, plants, and minerals are not merely means to ends. They are ends in themselves. They are not merely to be utilized and exploited, but rather, cared for. The human, the caretaker of God's kingdom, is responsible for their welfare, their fulfillment of God's highest and best intention for them.

God gave this command and authorization in the same universalistic context as He granted Adam the plants for food. That is to say that what applied there applies here as well; namely, that Adam is not merely a human but is the first human, and thus, at this point, the whole of humankind. Thus the responsibility and the authority for dominion-having or ruling over the creation is for all humans, at all times.[14] This means that all persons, in proportion to their abilities, should participate in this process. Some, of course, will have particular gifts of intellectual or leadership capability which will especially enable them to direct certain parts of the creation to its appointed ends. Others will have more limited scope for this stewardship but are equally responsible for what God gave them. This is the thrust of Jesus' stewardship parables. The man who had two talents was held as responsible for them as was the man with five for his, and the man with only one was rebuked for his failure to practice a good stewardship of that one.

In the setting of the original commission, the expression is in very concrete form: actual control of the plants and animals. Yet, this really involves anything pertaining to the organization, direction, and development of the whole world system, including politics, communication and much else besides. Thus, all human culture is derived from and dependent upon this.

One of the most difficult tasks of Christian social ethics is to determine exactly the legitimate limits of this stewardship. That is to say, when is this legitimate cultivation and fulfillment of the potential of the creation, and when does this represent this encroachment upon that creation? For example, do zoological parks properly express the harnessing and cultivating of creation as God intended, or do they improperly limit the freedom and activity of some of God's creatures? This will require some careful theological definitional work being done, to be sure. Similarly, most of us now regard slavery as wrong, since it greatly restricts the freedom of human beings, but what about government laws restricting various human activities? Should laws be enacted and enforced which restrict free choices by human beings, when such restriction actually helps a person realize and develop what that person ought to be?

In practice, we seem to show considerable variation, depending upon the issue. Most of us, for example, probably would argue, even theologically, that compulsory public school education is a good thing, at least up to a certain point or a certain level. It does help one realize his or her rational capacities. What, then, about a compulsory religious practice, such as mandatory worship, or mandatory prayer in public schools? Here we would probably tend to disagree. It is apparent that what we really need is a teleological definition both of humanity and of nature.

One need not be an Aristotelian in one's philosophy to see the value of a definition in terms of ends. Aristotle insisted that something really is not that which it is unless it fulfills its end or purpose.[15] Thus, a telephone being used as a paperweight is not really a telephone. We must understand the creation not only in terms of what it is in its natural, undisturbed or undeveloped condition but also in terms of what it could become. This is true of the human, as well.

Some aspects of what humans are intended to be can be fulfilled involuntarily on the person's part, while others must, by their very nature, be voluntary to be genuine. Requiring persons to eat (or feeding them intravenously), for instance, does not militate against the proper realization of the *telos*, even though the person might have chosen not to do so. On the other hand, some functions of the person cannot be commanded or coerced. One cannot be forced to love another, although one can be forced to do things that would be deemed loving if the correct motivation were present. Thus, religious devotion cannot be coerced. One cannot be made to love and glorify God, although he or she can be compelled to go through the motions of love.

7. One other very important issue concerns the nature, purpose, and destiny of human life. It is this: The true fulfillment, the true purpose of human life does not consist in accumulating wealth, or for that matter, fame, comfort, ease or any other kind of pleasure. It does not involve the "enjoyment of oneself" in the primary sense. This may seem at first to contradict one rather major set of biblical passages, especially as found in the Old Testament. There, wealth seem to indicate God's blessing. Some of God's most favored people were persons of substance. Abraham, a person with large flocks and herds, immediately comes to mind. Another is Job

(although his situation in life changed rather radically at one point in the narrative). Even the first Psalm seems to say that whatever a righteous person like Job does prospers, including presumably his economic situation.

Yet we must read the New Testament testimony alongside of this. Here several passages seem uniformly to support one major theme: that life is not primarily a matter of wealth and possessions. Jesus himself was not a well-to-do person. People have observed many times that His family did not even have the means to offer the usual purification sacrifice for a newborn infant. Instead of the usual lamb, they brought doves or pigeons (Luke 2:24; cf. Lev. 12:8). Jesus mentioned during His lifetime that although the birds of the air had their nests, and the foxes their holes, He did not have anywhere to lay His head (Matt. 8:20). In this, He seemed to contrast His status with what He promised His disciples (Matt. 6:32-33). On one occasion His disciples had nothing with which to pay the temple tax, and He commanded them to catch a fish. They found a coin in the fish's mouth and used it to pay the tax in question. If we hold that the life God really intended is the "good life"—doing well rather than doing good—then Jesus somehow missed God's intention for His children.

What Jesus taught by example He also taught more directly as well. He urged His hearers not to lay up for themselves treasures on earth, where moth and rust corrupt and thieves steal, but rather to lay up for themselves treasures in heaven, where they were not subject to such dangers (Matt. 6:19-20). He urged them not to be anxious about such matters as food and clothing. He even instructed one man to sell all that he had and give the proceeds to the poor, so that he might follow Jesus (Matt. 19:21). He stated that a man's life does not consist in the abundance of things (Luke 12:15). This theme runs through the remainder of the New Testament as well. The author of Hebrews urges us to be content with the things we have (Heb. 13:5). If we have food and clothing, we are to be content with that (1 Tim. 6:8).

We even must understand and evaluate the Old Testament

statements about wealth and God's blessing in the light of some of the statements about how we properly acquire these things and how we responsibly use them. Thus, the Old Testament prophets, especially Amos, condemn rich persons who acquire wealth through exploiting and oppressing the poor (e.g., Amos 5:11). While possessing wealth in itself may not be wrong, acquiring wealth by taking advantage of others is wrong, and failing to share one's wealth with deserving needy persons is wrong. Even the wealth possessed is not simply one's own, to be used exclusively on one's own self.

We now may summarize the biblical teaching as it bears upon this area of wealth. Quality of life is not a direct function of quantity of possessions. Wealth is not to be a major goal of one's life, and in particular, wealth acquired with disregard of the needs and welfare of the rest of the creation, especially of other humans, is wrong. Possessing wealth imposes special responsibilities upon those who have it, especially to use it to care for those less fortunate.

Understanding 'Be Fruitful'

8. One other major motif regarding humans needs to be developed here. It concerns the reproduction and multiplication of the human race. This becomes a factor in the other issues, for the number of persons which the environment must support or sustain affects the impact of the human upon that environment. Is there a biblical theology of human reproduction and population?

On the surface of things, it appears that the Bible gives no basis for limiting human reproduction. On the contrary, it seems more easily to justify maximum reproduction. Part of the very creation account itself was the command to be fruitful and multiply and fill the earth.

The Bible seems to describe children, like wealth, as a sign of God's blessing. Barrenness was a sign of God's withheld blessing (Sarah, Rachel, Hannah). Children, and large numbers of them, are taken to indicate God's blessing (Ps. 127:3-5).

How are we to understand this? Since wealth, which it seems

Scripture commends, does not seem quite so desirable when we examine the whole sweep of Scripture, perhaps it's also impossible to determine how desirable fecundity is when examined in this light.

We are attempting to determine whether the command to be fruitful and multiply and fill the earth is an absolute, universal, and permanent command, or a temporary, local, and limited command. To attempt to answer this question, we must look very closely at the original setting and then compare and contrast it with the current situation.

When God gave the command, He did so in the immediate context of the command to have dominion over or to subdue the earth. At that time, Adam was the entire human race. Being alone, it would be quite difficult or even impossible for him to accomplish this task. Not only was he alone, but he had no mechanization, automation or robotization. Agriculture, as it would be for many centuries, was labor-intensive. Further, the very survival of the human race depended upon its multiplying and doing so rapidly. Compared to the size of the human race at that point, the natural resources of the universe virtually were unlimited. Given the primitive state of technology, one pair's potential for polluting the universe was infinitesimal. That situation continued throughout basically all of biblical times. Population, relative to the earth and the task, was small. Also, children were both the work force in a largely agrarian society and the retirement and social security system, caring for the needs of the parents in old age.

If the command, however, was to "fill the earth," then it appears that it has been fulfilled. A sufficient population exists to inhabit the earth quite completely. Indeed, the opposite tendency, to overpopulate the earth, now is the great problem. A sufficient population now exists to direct and guide the creation, or to "have dominion" over it. Also, dominion-having presumably is a much less labor-intensive matter now than it was when God gave the original command. Mechanization of agriculture, for example, has greatly altered the ratio of workers to acres under cultivation.

Notes

1. Arnold Toynbee, "The Religious Background of the Present Environmental Crisis," *Ecology and Religion in History*, ed. David and Eileen Spring (New York: Harper & Row, 1974), 145-46.

2. Ian McHaig, *Design With Nature* (Garden City, NY: The National History Press, 1969), 26.

3. Lynn White, Jr., "The Historical Roots of our Ecological Crisis," *Western Man and Environmental Ethics*, ed. Ian Barbour (Reading, MA: Addison-Wesley, 1973), 43-54.

4. Wendell Berry; "A Secular Pilgrimage," *Western Man and Environmental Ethics*, 135.

5. Wesley Granberg-Michaelson, *A Worldly Spirituality: The Call to Redeem Life on Earth* (San Francisco: Harper & Row, 1984), 33-34.

6. Toynbee, "Religious Background," 149.

7. G. K. Chesterton, *The Everlasting Man* (London: Hodder and Stoughton, n.d.), 282.

8. Robert P. Meye, "Invitation to Wonder: Toward a Theology of Nature," *Tending the Garden: Essays on the Gospel and the Earth*, ed. Wesley Granberg-Michaelson (Grand Rapids: Eerdmans, 1987), 48.

9. Granberg-Michaelson, *A Worldly Spirituality*, 81-82.

10. Odil Hannes Steck, *World and Environment* (Nashville: Abingdon, 1980), 110.

11. Ibid., 46.

12. Granberg-Michaelson, *A Worldly Spirituality*, 78-79.

13. William Dymess, "Stewardship of the Earth in the Old Testament," *Tending the Garden*, 53-54.

14. Leonard Verduin, *Something Less Than God: The Biblical View of Man* (Grand Rapids: Eerdmans, 1970), 34-45.

15. Aristotle, *Metaphysics*, Book 2, chapter 2.

4

Humanistic and New Age Ideas and Ecological Issues

L. Russ Bush

Since the mid-1980s it has become clear that the New Age movement is a significant social-religious force in Western culture. It no longer merely is a subgroup of the larger occult-metaphysical community in the West. New Age philosophy now has taken the lead in the revival of the spiritualist tradition.

According to some researchers, most books and articles published about this movement appear to have been hostile critiques by evangelical Christians. Orthodox Christianity feels particularly threatened by this movement.

The New Age and the Rainbow

In 1984 Constance Cumbey, a trial lawyer from Detroit, published *The Hidden Dangers of the Rainbow*, a best-selling volume that introduced many people to the "conspiracy theory" version of the New Age movement.[1] According to Cumbey, the rainbow is the covert symbol members of the movement use to identify themselves secretly with one another (much as early Christians used the sign of the fish). She tried to persuade us that the New Age movement has eschatologically sinister intentions, that Christians need to be alert to the underlying unity of the seemingly diverse coalition. She implicitly warned that mainstream religious leaders were blind to the threat "New Agers" pose for American life.

Most observers today consider Cumbey's book to have been, at the least, simplistic. She was correct to sound a warning, but she did not grasp the true nature of New Age thinking. Many major figures openly advocate the New Age movement. It is not a hidden

55

conspiracy. Most often people present it as if it were an inevitable worldwide transformation of basic human consciousness levels, a new way of thinking that will affect and is affecting virtually all major people groups in modern cultures. This "new consciousness" seems to be a by-product of mass communication and contemporary media and technology. It definitely is a spiritual phenomenon, and it has explicit spiritual consequences.

No one has proved Cumbey's theory about the rainbow as a secret symbol to be correct, but she has pinpointed one of the most significant elements of modern New Age thinking—focus on the environment.[2]

What Is New About New Age?

Douglas R. Groothuis in 1986 presented one of the most significant of the early evangelical critiques of New Age thinking in his *Unmasking the New Age*.[3] He said people can sum up New Age philosophy in a single central thought: all is one.

Explore that central thought, and you come up with ideas like these: We are all god; the whole purpose of human life is to re-own the godlikeness within us; or as Shirley MacLaine puts it: Death does not exist; you have lived before and you will live again.

This is a new way of thinking for those in the West who always have seen death as the great enemy, the wages of sin, "the one-way street to the judgment seat." Jewish and Christian cultures always have made a clear distinction between people and God.

If "all is one," if we are god, and if the collective human mind is the ultimate reality, then we Christians have been fundamentally wrong about our whole way of thinking about the world and about life and about good and evil.

Poor us! We thought death was real. We thought the world was not God. We thought that a sovereign God made and controlled all. We thought God created *ex nihilo* and apart from Himself. We thought we were separated from those who were dead. We thought spiritualism and seances (now called channeling) were sinful and spiritually deceptive. We believed that we were not God, but we thought we were different from the animals. "New

Agers" tell us, however, that we have been holding onto an outdated world view. We have cut ourselves off from the harmonious dancing energy of the vital and mysterious universe.

Jim Henson, creator of the Muppets, was a strong advocate of this "New Age" viewpoint. Like Walt Disney, his main characters usually were self-conscious talking animals. Also like most of Disney's characters, Henson's creatures expressed humor and love and compassion for all "people."

We find Henson's most explicit statement of this "all-is-one" philosophy in his movie, *The Dark Crystal*. The Mystics and the Skeksis are the two types of "people" who rule the impoverished land. The "good" mystics spend their slow-moving lives chanting, caring for the necessities of their simple lifestyles, and thinking profound thoughts. The "evil" Skeksis, on the other hand, are hyperactive, shrill, gluttonous, power-hungry vultures who still live in the partially destroyed castle in the center of the land of darkness.

A little Gelfling discovers a piece of the magic crystal that stands in the center of the castle which is in the center of the land which is in the center of reality. It becomes the Gelfling's destiny to restore the unity of the magic crystal.

The movie is a masterpiece of puppetry. A dull moment never occurs, and the drama is exciting. At the last possible moment when proper astronomical conditions are just right, that one moment in time when everything in heaven and earth came together, the Gelfling, at great personal risk, restores the unity of the crystal. At the precise moment in eternity, the heavenly light is focused, and a fantastic transformation takes place. We discover that the Mystics and the Skeksis were not really good and evil but actually were incomplete parts of the same reality. They merge to become whole, and the land itself is transformed. No longer a desert, it now is verdant and moist.

Just as Luke Skywalker had to learn from Yoda that the Force is one, but that it has a good side and a dark side, and just as we all learn at the end that the "evil" Darth Vader in reality is a loving

Father, so George Lucas also has carried his New Age message into every home in America and into the minds of most of the young people of the Western world.

As a Christian, however, I must protest. Henson's and Lucas's world view is exactly the world view that would not, did not, and cannot produce the technologically advanced society that it presupposes. This "all-is-one" pantheism is the staple diet of ancient Hinduism and Buddhism.[4] Modern science grew and flourished, however, only in biblically based Christian cultures where the world was not seen as being filled with capricious spirits and deities, where the world was viewed as having been objectively created according to a rational plan and for a consistently implemented purpose. Those who still maintain a biblical world view expect that rationally discoverable patterns exist (we call them scientific principles or natural laws). This expectation, however, presupposes divine creation.[5]

The Need for a Biblical Base

The Christian world view never views all things as one. We believe two fundamentally different kinds of reality exist. One of those is God, the eternal, necessary Being; and the other is the world, a temporal collection of contingent beings. The latter exists because of the unique quality of the former's existence.

But let me draw out the logical implications of this new kind of thinking just a bit more. If "all is one," all might be impersonal matter. Personality might be nothing more than the grand illusion of complexity. This is the historic alternative to theism in the Western world: that humanity is the product of undirected evolution, that the mind is a product of chemical complexity and the "luck of the draw," so to speak. Impersonal energy arising from a quantum fluctuation, from an instability in an ancient black hole; impersonal matter resulting from a subsequent "Big Bang," and then from astral interiors that went nova; impersonal living organisms arising from a fortuitous lightning strike in the midst of an appropriate collection of gases, or from a random combination of chemicals near a thermal vent on the ocean floor; self-conscious personalities arising by means of natural elimination of the unfit random mutations that occur, thus leaving those best suited for survival in each successive environment; this is the scenario painted by naturalistic science. None of it is likely. All of it is improbable; yet, people believe it because seemingly the only alternative was to acknowledge God as the Maker of Heaven and Earth. Today, however, a "new" alternative has arisen.

Naturalism leads to meaningless existence. People who have been educated in this world view since kindergarten now see the stark reality of that. People are not mere animals. They cannot live in total meaninglessness. So if we are not merely naked apes, then what other alternatives exist?

Another ancient world view also exists. It is not biblical theism, but neither is it philosophical naturalism. It is spiritual monism: all is one, but all is not impersonal matter. Rather, "all is god."[6]

David K. Clark and Norman L. Geisler hit the nail right on the head in their recent book, *Apologetics in the New Age*. They subtitle the volume "A Christian Critique of Pantheism."[7] New Age thinking is anything but new. It is ancient pantheism in modern dress. It is mystical spiritualism and environmental holism. None of this is new, and none of this ultimately will satisfy the human longing for spiritual wholeness.

Matthew Fox, the controversial Dominican priest, advocated his brand of mystical spirituality as the answer to the world's cry for justice and liberation (something also claimed quite regularly as being the central meaning of rock music). Fox is deeply interested in "Mother Earth" and in the interaction of all religions on the planet. He claims Meister Eckhart and Teilhard de Chardin as spiritual mentors.[8] Harper and Row in 1988 published Fox's *The Coming of the Cosmic Christ: The Healing of Mother Earth and the Birth of a Global Renaissance*. Creation Spirituality, as he calls it, involves four ways of renewal: (1) Delight—the joyful respect for Mother Earth shown by sensual pleasures and eroticism; (2) Darkness—the silence of loneliness and suffering; (3) Birthing—

the liberating of the right-brain functions; and (4) Compassion—ecological concern, justice, and peacemaking.[9]

The fascinating right brain/left brain research has become a staple for New Age proponents. Left always is viewed as restrictive and unenlightened, while right-brain functions supposedly are good and are to be enhanced. But the more important aspect of Fox's work for our present purpose is his self-conscious personification of the physical world in which we live. The earth is our creator—our mother, according to Fox.

Fox is no absolute monist. He wants to distinguish good from evil so he can provide a basis for urging us to stop ravaging our "mother" with destructive behavior. But his spiritual environmentalism clearly is a modified monism in which God merely becomes the "soul" of the world, a being that relates to the world somewhat like an internal organ relates to the human body. Personal dialogue simply is not possible. This isn't the biblical God.[10]

Environmental concern almost never is biblically based today. We find it everywhere, however. Tom Cruise, hardly a religious figure, hosts Earth Day; John Denver establishes the Windstar Foundation; and media personalities all seem to be scrambling to be known as environmentalists. Christa Worthington's article in the April, 1991, issue of *Elle* magazine claims that the simplification of the ecological system will lead to a struggle for dominance. Humankind now is becoming a food species, she says. Malaria is back, and AIDS is an epidemic that only warns us of what is to come. Sea level is rising, global temperatures supposedly are rising, and oil fires in Iraq and Kuwait have polluted and poisoned our atmosphere.

But let me quote another section from Worthington's article: "The conservation movement is a religious force," writes John McPhea in his book on the guru of modern conservation, David Brower (formally of the Sierra Club and Friends of the Earth, now head of Earth Island Institute), a man of messianic purity who has

saved some of America's great rivers and canyons from water rec-
lamation (dams). "Environmentalism is driven by a totality of sen-
timent that borders on faith. . . ."

That faith is modified monism; it is Eastern religious mysticism;
it is pantheism; it is the Stephen Spielberg, George Lucas, Gene
Roddenberry, Walt Disney contribution to Western civilization.[11]
It is Hollywood and government, media and religion. This is the
New Age, and now we think differently about the world than did
any of our Christian ancestors.[12]

A Biblical Response to Environmental Issues

At the risk of ridicule from those who have decided that God's
Word speaks only to spiritual (translate that: personal, individual,
subjective, experiential, and existential) matters, and therefore
that it is not without error in matters of ordinary history or in
descriptions of nature, I nevertheless venture a few thoughts that
any straightforward reading of the biblical text seems to demand. I
mean no harm in this, and I hope that the simplicity of my points
will not offend those who seek "deeper meanings" in their biblical
expositions.

First of all, the Genesis account of creation is a classic biblical
narrative, giving every internal evidence of being fully historical.
The garden God prepared is located in the East, in Eden. This
geographical identification refers to the flat plain east of the promised land, east of Palestine, in the region near the Tigris and Eu-
phrates Rivers. The place was a real place prepared for human
habitation. Though we cannot pinpoint the exact location, we can
note that the Bible describes a specific location.

Next, we note that God created Adam before God prepared the
garden. Genesis 2:8 is rather explicit in saying not that God made
Adam in the garden, but God now "put" in the garden the human
He made in v. 7. Then v. 15 reaffirms this "putting," and then
comes the purpose statement. Why did God do this? Why did He
prepare a place? To provide a suitable environment with food and

with wildlife, an environment that could have provided humankind with protection. What is the human being to do who is put there? The answer is equally explicit: to work it and take care of it.

Can we not see how important the historicity of this narrative is to our theology? What is the function of humankind here on earth? Not what must it do because of sin (though that has environmental consequences as well), but what must it do even in a non-fallen world, even in the garden of Eden? People must work the garden and keep it. The agriculturalist, the farmer, and the rancher represent the heart of any nation. We can do without oil, but we cannot do without food and shelter.

God wants people not only to work the garden and help things to grow but also to take care of it, to protect it. The garden needed protection. It needed protection from Satan's entrance (a task, by the way, in which people failed). But it also needed protection from destruction by wildlife, human overpopulation, and pollution. At the same time, God commands Adam to reproduce and one day to fill the earth with descendants. God's garden needed environmental protection, but it also needed expansion and growth. The earth was a natural resource for people, a source of health and wealth.

We no longer live in that garden. Our earth is under judgment, and it groans as it waits for redemption (Rom. 8:19-22). It still needs, however, the protection that only humans can offer. The earth is the Lord's, but we are His people, in His image, caring for an environment cursed due to our sin. All the more reason to support reasonable efforts to sustain the environment!

But look at how different this is from New Age concerns. Biblically, we are not the products of evolution. We are not caring for nature as if the earth were our mother or our god. We are caring for our environment because God placed us here for that purpose even before sin. Because of sin, we have an even greater obligation because we feel responsible for the world that was judged along with us in the Fall's aftermath. As true servants of the Creator, we care for and wisely use the earth to produce food and energy for all humankind. We care for the earth not because it is a living being but because it is our home, a gift of God for our good, a source of revelation (Rom. 1:20), and a manifestation of God's glory (Ps. 19).

Adam's offspring work the soil and raise domestic animals. Noah, by God's grace, survives an environmentally catastrophic judgment on human sin. The rainbow, in fact, stands as the covenant symbol of God's environmental protection policy (Gen. 9:8-17). Moreover, a green rainbow of life encircles the throne of God in heaven (Rev. 4:3). How much more clearly could the Bible speak?

The Christian World View and Environmental Concerns

Pantheism destroys meaning and human values. Pantheism is not true despite its wide acceptance in Eastern religions. Biblical creationism is true. We love the Lover, and thus we love that which the Lover has made.

We believe that just as water will quench thirst, a true world view will meet humankind's deepest needs. Only the truth ultimately will satisfy.

People look for truth. Christianity not only is a strong world view that we can test and is not afraid of the evidence, but it is also practically relevant. It meets human needs. It provides purpose and direction for human life, and it solves human problems such as guilt. It enables human beings to establish meaningful relationships. It relates them to the world as the world really is.[13]

One reason the energy crisis has become so serious is that we have not dealt with nature as managers handling something God created, but we have acted as if nature simply were a machine. We have pushed a button here and expected the machine to operate and produce over there. Yet nature is not and never has been only a physical machine. We cannot treat it that way, or we will destroy it.

We cannot build highways just anywhere purely on the basis of human desires or convenience. We must recognize that the earth is a complex, interdependent ecological system. It should be properly managed.

Human beings are to have dominion in the sense of being those who control nature and rule over it for the purpose of making it useful and making it productive. But we have treated nature as if it were an impersonal, material, purely physical system that we could handle without any concern about a possible moral relationship to it.

Nature is not a purposeless machine. It is a system of physical energy/matter God created to accomplish His purpose(s). Human society has reached a crisis in dealing with nature, because people have thought about nature from an incorrect world view.

Human society and family relationships seem to be breaking down. Why? Because society has dealt with people not as personalities created in the image of God but as highly complex, sophisticated animals, consumers, or biological machines. Human beings do respond to stimuli. Our environment affects us. But that is not the end of the story. People are not merely animals. We do more than consume energy. We are not machines. We are spiritual beings whom God created in His personal image.

Christianity is a world view which, because of who people are, demands meaningful human relationships and proper social structures and strong families. Human relationships are built upon and from divine relationships. In these ways and in a thousand similar ways, Christianity has practical relevance.[14]

Humanism and New Age pantheism live in an environment of illusion. By fundamentally misunderstanding what the world is, these world views ultimately are out of touch with reality. As Christians, we may have many common concerns with environmental activists, but we always must stand for biblical truth. God is the only necessary Being. The universe as a whole and each of its parts are equally incomplete. All created reality is contingent, temporal, and subject to decay and loss. Only Christ can save us. He and He alone knows all, cares completely, and has promised to bring about an unparalled ecological cleansing in His own time and in His own way. Even so come, Lord Jesus.

Notes

1. See Constance Cumbey, *The Hidden Dangers of the Rainbow* (Lafayette, LA: Huntington, 1984).

2. The "Subject Guide" of *Books in Print 1990-1991* lists almost 14 pages of titles under "Environment" (and subheads). "New Age" has over 170 titles (though only three seemed explicitly to be related to nature and/or the environment.) Under "Man-Influence on Nature" I found 72 titles, but none seemed to be by evangelicals or, to my knowledge, even Christian authors. "Nature (in Religion, Folklore, etc.)" listed only 10 titles; a couple were historical works, one was on all the birds in the Bible, one was on all the flowers in the Bible, a couple were Jewish works, one was a Catholic work and only Margaret Clarkson's *All Nature Sings* seems to have come from a generally evangelical publisher (Eerdmans). Southern Baptists need to do and say more in this area, but we should note that environmental concerns are explicitly addressed in Chapter 6 of the Member's Booklet from the Equipping Center Module: *Facing the Future: A Christian Response* (Nashville: Sunday School Board of the SBC, 1989). The most comprehensive and objective source of information to date on the New Age movement is found in J. Gordon Melton's *New Age Encyclopedia: A Guide to the Beliefs, Concepts, Terms, People, and Organizations That Make up the New Global Movement Toward Spiritual Development, Health and Healing, Higher Consciousness, and Related Subjects* (Detroit: Gale Research, 1990). An appendix lists well over 50 American and Canadian institutions that offer fully accredited graduate and/or undergraduate degree programs in New Age studies. These include the University of Oklahoma, Indiana University, University of Alabama, University of Maryland, Syracuse University, University of South Florida, and many others.

3. See Douglas R. Groothuis, *Unmasking the New Age* (Downers Grove: InterVarsity, 1986).

4. As a well-known example of the influence of Eastern philosophical ideas on New Age "science" see Fritjof Capra, *The Tao of Physics* (Boulder: Shambhala, 1975).

5. Clearly evolutionary theories also assume natural law, but philosophical naturalism becomes, at best, purposeless and, at worst, meaningless. These laws ("regularities") have no foundation; they ultimately rest upon principles of "indeterminacy"; and they cannot justify the validity of rational inference. See L. Russ Bush, *A Handbook for Christian Philosophy* (Grand Rapids: Zondervan, 1991) for a more detailed development of this argument.

6. The New Age desire for a transformation of human consciousness expresses

itself in at least three ways. Holism is the central term. Whether the issue is health, life-style, human rights, or the environment, the relevant focus is the holistic one. This quite naturally leads to an emphasis on earth awareness because the earth is one of the most important "systems" of which we are a part. Brazilian rain forests are of prime concern, but nuclear radiation, industrial waste, and other pollutants are the enemy of the system and must be resisted at all costs and at all levels. New Agers see every local issue as a part of the global concern. The most dramatic expression of this is the so-called "Gaia" hypothesis: the view that the earth is a living entity and humanity is a vital part of the earth's life (somewhat like microbes that are essential to human life).

7.   See David K. Clark and Norman L. Geisler, *Apologetics in the New Age* (Grand Rapids: Baker, 1990). Interestingly enough, their section on "Exposition of New Age Pantheism" treats Spinoza and Plotinus as well as Suzuki, Shankara, and Radhakrishnan. Common New Age themes suggested by Clark and Geisler include: the oneness of reality; the impersonality of God; creation out of God by necessity; the divinity of human beings; levels of reality merely as expressions of levels of perceptional ignorance; knowledge by direct apprehension; the inadequacy of language and logic and only intuition as being self-certifying. Intuition is thus deified. Knowledge, then, is salvation, and ignorance is the source of evil. But the knowledge sought is not rational knowledge; it is the mystical experience of enlightenment: something like Indiana Jones' father claimed to find when the water from the holy grail was poured into his mouth and over his physical wounds. His miraculous healing symbolized the illusory nature of good and evil, pain and sorrow. This is the essence of New Age thinking. (From the final sequence in Stephen Spielberg's movie *Indiana Jones and the Last Crusade*.)

8.   See Robert Brow, "The Taming of the New Age Prophet," *Christianity Today* (June 16, 1989), 28-30. In 1980 Fox published *Breakthrough: Meister Eckhart's Creation Spirituality, in new translation* (Garden City: Doubleday, 1980).

9.   See also Matthew Fox, *A Spirituality Named Compassion and the Healing of the Global Village, Humpty Dumpty, and Us* (Minneapolis: Winston, 1979).

10.   Some of Matthew Fox's other relevant works include: *On Becoming a Musical, Mystical Bear: Spirituality American Style* (New York: Paulist, 1976); *Whee! We, Wee all the Way Home: A Guide to Sensual, Prophetic Spirituality* (Santa Fe: Bear & Co., 1981).

11.   Spielberg virtually has single-handedly reversed Western thought patterns regarding beings from outer space (a major theme in New Age literature). No longer are space creatures monsters who destroy Tokyo or New York. Now they are saviors and friends (cf. *ET* and *Close Encounters of the Third Kind*). Lucas has established the mysticism of the East as the dominant philosophy of the universe at large. *Star Wars* is not a movie about our future but about our past.

12.   One of the best sources for reviewing the New Age movement (though the

impact of New Age thinking on environmentalism is not prominent in the book) is Russell Chandler's *Understanding the New Age* (Dallas: Word, 1988). Interestingly enough, Francis Schaeffer seems to have been well ahead of his time when he published *Pollution and the Death of Man* in 1970. See *The Complete Works of Francis A Schaeffer: A Christian World View*, Vol. 5 (Westchester: Crossway, 1982). He included as an appendix Lynn White, Jr.'s "The Historical Roots of Our Ecological Crisis."

13. Out of many excellent studies on this subject, I mention only Colin A. Russell's *Cross-currents: Interaction between Science and Faith* (Grand Rapids: Eerdmans, 1985).

14. See Bush, *Handbook*, 90-91.

III
The Ethical Application

5

Biblical Ethics of Ecology
Millard J. Erickson

We tend to think of the ecological problem as something relatively recent in origin. Actually, it has been with us for a long time.

Here are some examples of this: In A. D. 61, the Roman poet Seneca wrote, "As soon as I had gotten out of the heavy air of Rome and from the stink of the smoky chimneys thereof, which, being stirred, poured forth whatever pestilent vapors and soot they held enclosed in them, I felt an alteration of my disposition." In 1257, Eleanor of Aquitane, the queen of Henry II, moved from Nottingham to Tutbury Castle to get away from what she termed "the undesirable smoke." In 1661, the diarist John Evelyn described the "hellist and dismal cloud of sea coal" and its unhealthful effects upon London residents.[1]

Recently, however, with the rapid population growth and industrialization, these problems have grown greatly. As Christians, we are responsible for alleviating this condition.

Having developed briefly in Chapter 3 a theology of ecology, we now turn to implementing this in terms of an ethic of ecology. This first requires that we state something about how we understand theology, Christian ethics, and our ethical methodology.

Applying the Bible to Life

The very nature of the Christian faith, as we understand it, is that belief and action or living are very closely connected. We see this in Jesus' metaphor of the tree and its fruit, culminating in His statement, "Why do you call me, 'Lord, Lord,' and do not do what I say?" (Luke 6:46, NIV). We see this in numerous other places in the Bible as well, however. Paul repeatedly applies to ethical living the theological truth he has expounded. We see this, for example, in the way in which his statement in Ephesians 2:10, NIV that "we are God's workmanship, created in Christ Jesus to do good works" follows the well-known statement in verses 8 and 9 about having been saved by grace through faith.

Sometimes the application precedes the statement of doctrine, so that the doctrine is introduced as the justification for the command. This occurs in Philippians 2:1-11, where Christ's attitude and conduct commands the believer's behavior. We find the crux of the argument in v. 5, NIV. "Your attitude should be the same as that of Christ Jesus." Even the Old Testament law rested upon such a conception: "I am the Lord your God; consecrate yourselves and be holy, because I am holy" (Lev. 11:44, NIV).

We should notice, however, that the Bible does not simply restrict this behavior to one's action in relationship to God, or to religious behavior. To be sure, the first and great commandment that the Old Testament gives us and Jesus affirms is to love the Lord with all one's being (Mark 12:30). The second, which Jesus said is like it (Matt. 22:39), is to love one's neighbor as oneself (Mark 12:31). He said no greater command exists than these (Mark 12:31). Thus, He linked the command about how to treat others as being on the same level of importance with the command to love God.

This distinguishes Christianity from some other religions in which theology and ethics are separated. In such approaches, one may derive his or her ethic from other, more secular sources, or may simply adopt it from one's surrounding society. For orthodox or evangelical Christianity, however, our Christian theology's content definitely impacts our Christian ethics.

We need to note that Christians currently practice several different types of ethical methodology. We may term one general approach "legalism." This attempts to reduce the issues of Christian ethics to laws dictating behavior. These are understood to be universal or unexceptionable in character. They always apply, everywhere and to everyone. We often understand these to come directly from Scripture, so that the character of the biblical revelation is that we have received laws or rules. We simply are to follow these laws because of how the Bible reveals them.

This view does credit to the fact that biblical revelation does not merely present a person but communicates truth—propositional truth. God has both informed us about the truth and directed us about the good and the right. It also takes into account God's absoluteness and supremacy. He alone has the right to prescribe what is true and right. Thus, the wishes of humans or any other members of the creation do not have to be factored in when determining what is right.

This approach, however, has two major shortcomings. One is that it fails to take into account the specific or localized character of much of the biblical revelation. In many cases, Scripture does not give its ethical dictums as universal statements about all situations one might ever encounter but as responses to specific situations. This rule or law might not be given if the situation had been slightly different.

Closely related to this is the fact that God gave many different commands. Some may have applied both to that original situation and to the present one at hand, and others applied or apply only to one or the other. We even see this in the distinctions Scripture draws between different members of a general class of actions. For example, according to the Bible, is it right or wrong to kill another human being? The Bible gives rather differing answers to that question. On the one hand, in what seems to be a universal statement, God prohibits taking human life: "Whoever sheds the blood of man, by man shall his blood be shed; for in the image of God has God made man" (Gen. 9:6, NIV).

Yet elsewhere, the Bible permits killing, in cases of a murderer. It was for this reason that cities of refuge were commanded, so that persons would not be able to exercise their justifiable right to take vengeance (Num. 35:1-15). Further, in situations such as war and capital punishment, killing another human was not merely permissible but mandatory. This was command, not concession. It appears from such considerations that many more laws existed than people first realized, or that the law governing taking or not taking human life must be much more complex than people formerly believed.

Another possible explanation exists which accounts for this variation. This other explanation is that no absolute or divinely revealed laws exist. The divine command is not to do a certain thing but to act in a certain fashion or to do whatever one does with a certain attitude or motivation. This accounts for the apparent contradiction on a cognitive or propositional basis, for that is not the true locus of divine will for humans. From this, various types of relativistic ethics have emerged. The most prominent of these recently has been situation ethics.

Situation ethics maintains that nothing is always right or wrong, good or bad. What makes something good is whether it is the most loving thing to do. If, in a given situation, a particular action is the most loving thing to do, then it is good and right. If, on the other hand, it is not the most loving thing to do, it is bad and wrong. The only thing that always is good is love, and the only action that always is right is to act in the most loving fashion. This approach places normativity in an attitude or a way of doing things, rather than in specific content or things to be done. It sees God as having revealed not what to do but how to be.[2]

The value of this approach lies in its having seen the complexity of the moral situation. The apparent contradictions found among the divine commands indicate the variety of values involved in the typical ethical decision or directive. It correctly fixes normativity in a principle, that of love, but makes the mistake of restricting ethical considerations to that one principle.

Seeking Solutions

A third approach to ethical decision-making is one I believe incorporates the strengths of these approaches while avoiding the difficulties and errors of each. Rather than legalistic or situational, I would term this approach "principial." It maintains that the locus of divine revelation and thus of normativity is the ethical principle. This does not in any sense deny the idea of verbal inspiration but maintains that in matters of ethics, the words are the vehicle for conveying the principles God intends for humans to know and honor. The rules given in differing situations varied because different combinations of principles applied. The Christian ethicist's task, therefore, is to determine what principles apply to the given case under consideration and to combine them in a way producing a rule governing action in cases of this type.

This means that indeed an objective—good or bad, right or wrong—exists for each situation, but the rule expressing it may be much more complex than some have thought. We will seek to follow this ethical methodology in the rest of this chapter. Chapter 3 was designed to detect and expose those theological motifs constituting the values appropriate to the issues of ecological ethics. We now will attempt to draw upon those values as principles and to identify the ones which, in the appropriate combination, will give us action directives.

In our discussion we must bear in mind one additional major distinction between what we might term ethical solutions and practical solutions. Another way of describing these might be to term them the strategic and the tactical solutions. The ethical solution or the strategic solution describes the state of affairs that we decide is desirable or is the solution to the ethical problem. The practical solution or the tactical solution, however, represents the specific actions or procedures necessary to bring about the ethical or strategic solution. Sometimes the impracticality of the former makes the realization of the latter quite difficult.

A story from World War II illustrates the point. Early in the war, German submarines, frequently operating in wolf packs, were sinking large numbers of American cargo ships, making it difficult to supply our military personnel and our allies with the supplies necessary for successfully carrying on the war. Much thought and anguish went into attempting to stop this heavy attrition. Finally one man proposed what he thought to be a brilliant solution. "Heat the water of the Atlantic Ocean to 212 degrees," he said. "When the German U-boats surface, we can simply pick them off with guns and bombs."

"That is a brilliant idea," someone responded, "but how would you heat that much water?"

"Don't ask me," replied the man. "I just make policy; I don't carry it out."

In terms of our analysis, the general value or principle pursued was ending the loss of U.S. cargo ships. The strategic solution was destroying the German submarines. The tactical solution was heating the water to force the submarines to surface.

Taking the Matter Seriously

Often another complicating factor is that many different values which we may want to preserve exist, and preserving or maximizing one may be possible only through endangering or minimizing another. Single-issue persons seldom see this dilemma. We need to bear in mind that differing on the tactical or practical solution does not mean that we do not accept the same ethical solution as the other person. It simply may mean that we do not find the practical solution effective or that we espouse additional principles which we also believe to be affected by this course of action.

Let us say, for example, that we concluded that polluting the environment—specifically polluting the atmosphere by smokestack emissions—is a bad thing, and further, that all such emissions should be terminated and prohibited immediately. If we were to do that, however, some severe ramifications would occur. Many, many persons would become unemployed. Modifying the manufacturing processes necessary to effect the requisite emissions reduction would increase the manufacturing cost of these products considerably, thus increasing inflation measurably. Either or both of these effects in turn significantly would impact the economy. Thus, we must seek to arrive at some ethical solutions and then begin searching for the best possible practical solutions.

Our discussion here primarily will focus upon ethical solutions, but to illustrate, we will carry the discussion of the first ethical solution to elaborate on possible practical solutions.

1. We must seek to preserve the purity, beauty, and integrity of all creation. More specifically, we must find ways to reduce, and as nearly as possible eliminate, the pollution of our environment, that is to say, the entire creation. We must endeavor to reduce the harmful emissions into the air, water, and soil.

For us as individual, believing Christians, that means we will take great care to ensure that we are not contributing to the pollution of our world and universe. Using certain substances and avoiding others will help to advance that cause. Even if it means foregoing some economic advantage or some element of convenience, we will choose practices and substances which are environmentally healthy.

This is a matter of personal ethics, what we as individuals do. It would help considerably if every Christian in our country took seriously his or her own stewardship of the environment. Given the number of Christians, or even the number of evangelical Christians in the United States, this would impact the environment measurably.

Beyond that, however, we will be concerned about our social ethics; by that we mean not only our individual actions but those of the society. Social ethics for the individual Christian represents his or her efforts to influence on a societal scale what is done.

We can accomplish some of this through economic and other forms of influence. Boycotting certain types of products or those of certain corporations which pollute the environment can be quite effective. Resolutions by national church bodies are not noted to be effective in altering corporate policy, but if the members of such a denomination back these resolutions up with actions, demonstrating how serious their intent is, this could be considerably influential.

Suppose, for example, that the Southern Baptist Convention, in its annual assembly, passed a resolution censuring the manufacture and distribution of a certain very polluting product. After this, the SBC notified the manufacturer of the resolution and urged the manufacturer to stop producing the product. If, after adequate opportunity, the corporation involved failed to comply, the congregations would be informed of this nonconformity. Since the messengers already had alerted the congregations about the annual assembly's action, the congregations would be prepared to take action. The congregations would vote to urge their members to boycott the offending party. The SBC also would inform the offending manufacturer's competitors that it would monitor and respond to any attempt to use such a boycott as an opportunity to raise prices.

Think of the message such an action would send! The regional managers for the sections of the country where Southern Baptists are especially numerous soon would be able to verify how serious the action was. Their sales figures would reveal that.

What of those cases where not merely one company but all in a given field are offending? Even if Southern Baptists could persuade one manufacturer to change its product and all the Southern Baptists turned their patronage toward that one brand, success probably would not be achieved. The reason is that the different process adopted probably would put that manufacturer at an economic disadvantage over others. Often manufacturing a nonpolluting product is more costly than manufacturing the polluting version, which is why companies are not manufacturing the nonpolluting in the first place. That would leave the good guys on the horns of an economic dilemma. They might sell at a competitive price but would suffer a considerably diminished level of profit or even a loss. That would hamper the corporation and eventually would probably drive it out of manufacturing that product. The alternative would be to raise prices to reflect the increased cost of manufacture. If this, however, made that brand more expensive than competitors' product, persons not involved in the boycott (and, unfortunately, probably some who were) would purchase the competing brands, thus also penalizing and possibly crippling the complying manufacturer. Thus, the endeavor would seem to prove self-defeating.

Another approach may be effective in such situations. That is to follow a technique such as the United Auto Workers union uses in negotiating labor contracts with the Big Three auto companies. Here one of the three is targeted for negotiations and, if a satisfactory agreement is not reached, is struck. Once settlement is reached, the other two companies generally go along with that agreement, but if not, a second company could be struck. It would seem that singling out one manufacturer for boycott would send a sufficiently strong message to the others, but if that is not effective, a rotation of the boycott could follow.

In some cases, however, the procedure outlined above is not adequate to solve the problem. This, then, would call for different means. That means we would need certain laws passed forbidding certain practices. We also would need a further commitment to strict enforcement of existing and future laws. It would not always be necessary to outlaw absolutely the offending practice or substance. If someone attaches penalties to the undesirable action or charges fees for the consequences (as for waste disposal), making the undesirable action more expensive or less profitable than the desired action, large corporations will modify how they conduct their businesses. This employs a combination of legal and economic means.

This means we must understand clearly the different senses of the world as an expression in Scripture. Christopher Derrick has pointed out that St. Francis was both the least worldly and the most worldly of individuals.[3] He certainly had learned to live the "separated life." He was a person of simplicity, of self-denial. Yet his love for the world, in terms of the created universe and all forms of life within it, is legendary. The created world is not inherently evil; it is inherently good, while the world, as the system of ungodly values and structures, is inherently evil. We must learn to love the former while we hate the latter.

Further, we must love the world in the former sense with the right type of love. It helps to distinguish between love as *eros* and love as *agape*. If our love for the creation is an *eros* type of love, then we will want to possess it, to exploit it, to consume it. That type of love has contributed to our current ecological crisis. If, on the other hand, we love the creation with a concern and care for its welfare, for what we can do to maximize its potential, then we love with an *agape* love. And the preponderance of *agape* over *eros* in the relationship to all objects of God's *agape* love is what distinguishes Christians, it seems to me.

Taking Care for God's Sake

2. We must act to maintain ourselves for the glory of God. By this we mean our total health: physical, psychological, and emotional, as well as the full development of ourselves for the sake of the kingdom of God. We will seek physical health through such means as careful diet and exercise and preventive and corrective medicine. Practicing good principles of mental hygiene also will be part of this. Developing our gifts and aptitudes through education and practice will be an act of stewardship. This will involve one's occupation, hobbies and service for the Lord. "Be all that you can be" is not simply a slogan of a branch of the military service. It is a maxim of the believer. Since we are part of the creation, and a very important part at that, we will want to take good care of ourselves. This may seem at first glance to be a self-centered approach, but it is a case of loving oneself, not for one's own sake, but for God's sake.

3. We also must commit ourselves to carefully conserving and consuming our creation's resources. This means that we find ways to use less of the energy resources and the raw materials of manufacture. All of these are finite in amount. When we mine and remove the iron ore within the earth's shell, no more will exist. When we exhaust the petroleum, coal, and natural gas deposits, no more will exist. (The processes by which fossil fuels were formed are still occurring but at such a rate relative to our rate of consumption as to be virtually negligible.) When the aluminum, lead,

zinc, nickel, and other resources are gone, they are irreplaceable. Yet, by no means can we be certain that the human race still will not need these materials. The Christian has a significant stake in assuring that we do not find the machine of the human race attempting to run with some of its crucial gauges registering "empty."

We are concerned about several elements in this matter. One is simply reducing the amount of items we consume. In our society, we have necessary and optional expenditures. Some of our necessary expenditures are relatively more efficient and others are relatively less efficient. We need to ask which of these are really necessary and to what degree. We also want to utilize the varieties that are more efficient than others. This might mean many things: limiting our trips to those with a justifiable purpose; buying smaller, more fuel-efficient automobiles; car-pooling; taking public transportation rather than driving our own vehicles; using refillable or recyclable rather than disposable products; and purchasing more durable, albeit more expensive, items, reducing the need for early or frequent replacement.

A further dimension is through the use of renewal resources. For example, utilizing wood products rather than plastic will enable us to replace the source of the raw material. We must accompany this with sound methods of forest and timber management. In the process, we will in many cases use biodegradable materials versus those not biodegradable.

Closely related to this is harnessing energy sources which currently are going to waste and which will continue to do so if we don't use them. One of these which we learned to exploit rather early in the industrial age is hydroelectric power. Today, however, we have numerous other parallels to such technology. The wind, for example, is a nearly continuous manifestation of power that simply is wasted. Abandoned windmills across our land testify to this wise use of wind power before abundant inexpensive energy was available. I grew up on a farm where we drank and bathed with water pumped by a windmill and listened to a radio powered by a storage battery which was charged by a wind-operated generator on our roof. I can assure you it is not nostalgia but a concern for our world's resources that causes me to call on us to consider increased use of wind, tidal, solar, and other forms of energy utilization.

It may seem as if we Americans are only a small part of the world's population (currently about 5 percent and growing relatively smaller) and therefore can do little to affect the situation of the world. Yet, make no mistake about it: We are the ones most in need of changing our behavior patterns.

When I taught Christian social ethics, an unusual measurement was quite convenient in dealing with these matters. The Indian equivalent was the number of residents of India that equaled one citizen of another country in terms of consumption of natural resources and pollution of the environment. At that time, the Indian equivalent of one American was 40, meaning that one of us consumed and polluted as much as 40 Indians. The other developed nations, of course, share in this same problem much as we do, but we head the list. We may take some pride in the fact that we are controlling our population growth much better than are the undeveloped and the developing nations, but that should be small comfort to us, in light of our rate of assault upon the creation.

Closely allied to this is the fact that we need to emphasize reusing, reprocessing, or recyling materials. Here consumer pressure has begun to affect the practices of some corporations, such as fast- food chains' shift to cardboard rather than Styrofoam containers. Municipalities have passed recycling ordinances and made available the means for recycling.

We should note that in some of these endeavors we have the possibility of effecting what I term a double-plus solution, reducing both consumption and pollution at the same time. One of the tensions of ethics is that sometimes we solve one problem only to create another. Sometimes, however, solving one problem also can help solve another. For example, some cities have ordinances keeping sanitary landfills from accepting leaves, since the plastic bags used to ship leaves to landfills would not degrade for many, many years. Meanwhile, landfills were becoming exhausted as sources of disposal. Municipal compost heaps represent a solution to this. They provide increased fertility of soil while keeping landfills from being clogged. Responsible Christians will support ordinances like banning leaves at landfills and will cooperate fully with these ordinances.

How Our Life-styles Affect the Creation

4. We must be willing to accept a lower individual standard of living for ourselves, for the sake of society or of the entire creation. Some courses of action this chapter discusses will add to the cost of things. That means we will not be able to afford quite as much of something as we would otherwise. For example, if the cost of recycling something is incorporated into its selling price, that price undoubtedly will increase.

Yet this may not actually affect our "standard of living" as much as we may think. The term which we should probably utilize is "quality of life" rather than standard of living. What is the quality of life, when the air is so polluted that on certain days citizens are advised to avoid vigorous physical activity causing them to deeply inhale polluted air? What is the quality of life, if polluting water results in more deaths, earlier deaths, or poorer health than otherwise would be the case? Even from the perspective of enlightened self-interest, these steps may not reduce but actually may amplify the quality of life.

Another dimension exists to this. Are we willing to see the costs of what we consume increased, if thereby others' health and prosperity increases? Are we willing to oppose the policies of multinational corporations which make their goods less expensive to us, but by paying an absolutely minimum and impoverishing wage to workers of other countries which supply the raw materials or the finished products? Are we willing to insist that companies follow practices which will help guarantee the safety and the health of their workers, even if that costs us more? Here we move to share the wealth and even the health with others, insisting on a little less for ourselves.

5. All of this means, further, that we should commit ourselves to simplicity of life versus materialism. It means simply getting along with fewer "things." This will have three benefits, or perhaps more accurately, three beneficiaries.

First, we should adopt this life-style because of what it will do for and to the creation. It will mean that we will consume less of its natural resources and pollute it less, for both consumption and pollution are concerned with physical or material objects.

Moreover, we should adopt this life-style because of what it does to others. When we do not consume these resources and do not despoil the creation, these things are available to others. This includes other persons in our world currently as well as future generations. We noted in the earlier chapter that God gave all persons the creation and charged them with stewardship or dominion over it. He did not just give this to Adam and Eve. None of us knows how many generations yet will exist upon our earth. The less we consume, the more will be left for others. We must make certain that our social ethic functions on at least as high a level as our social etiquette. Certainly none of us would think of taking so much food for ourselves that some guests at the meal would get none. That is the theory behind "seconds"—that one does not take all one can possibly eat, at the first opportunity, but only takes the additional amount after all have had some. Yet, if we consume mindlessly without thinking about those who are to come after us, we may display a more serious lack of concern for others.

This very analogy should offer us another clue or suggestion about how we solve our problems. We need increasingly to think of members of the world's population as being our friends and brothers and sisters. If we saw a member of our family or a good friend in need, we certainly would be moved by that need and would do something to help. If we realized that our own actions were causing that situation, we certainly would feel responsible.

That does not necessarily extend to persons far away and of a different culture, however. Their hunger may not affect our greed, which may contribute to it. We may grieve over the casualties our forces suffer in a war while we fail to realize that the casualties on the other side are equally serious and bring the same type of sorrow to the families of those killed and wounded. We need to pray that God will create in us a sense of unity with all of the human race, and beyond that, with the rest of the creation.

This will require us to transform our attitudes about material things and their use. In both the Old Testament and the New, we see a dimension of the idea of joyful sharing of what one had.[4] We often see that fundamental realities are spiritual rather than material. In the material realm, what I give to others at least seems to reduce what I have myself. Thus, if I have $100 and give $50 to someone else, I have only $50 remaining. If, however, we perform an act of kindness, we do not decrease what we have or are, we increase it. A compliment, a kind word spoken, an act of assistance makes us a kinder person, brings us happiness in giving happiness to others.[5]

Part of this will involve a broadened understanding of what salvation really is, what we really are saved from. This in turn will depend upon an expanded concept of sin. Part of what Christ saves us from is selfishness, with its insatiable desires for self-satisfaction. Also, He delivers us from conformity, with the seeming need to "keep up with the Joneses." Much of the consumption that is contributing to our ecological problems occurs when we desire something simply because others have it. When we fully grasp the depth and scope of salvation, it will help make us part of the solution rather than part of the problem.[6]

Living Simply to Enjoy Life More

Finally, we should commit ourselves to simplicity of life because of what it will do to us. Unfortunately, materialism causes us to lose enjoyment in the little things of life. I have thought about this while riding my bicycle to work and hearing the beauty of birds' songs all around me. I found that bicycle riding was one of those nearly perfect activities. I could get exercise, transportation, devotions (so long as I did not close my eyes while praying) and entertainment all at once, while saving money and only spending about an additional ten minutes of time each one-way trip.

Yet also around me were joggers who ran with portable radios or players attached to their belts and headphones on their ears. I do not know what they were listening to, but they were missing the beauty of the birds' song and also were endangering themselves by drowning out the sound of approaching vehicles. The money not spent on a "walkman" was in this case money well unspent, for it placed me back in contact with the simple beauty of nature. The person who must spend time and money receiving stimulation on a video game has lost the ability to enjoy the beauty of butterflies and flowers. We often require greater and greater stimulation, often artificial in nature, in order to find satisfaction. Materialism robs us of a certain element of our humanity.[7]

The Christian is one who basically maintains that the real satisfactions in life are spiritual in nature. If that is the case, then we really do not need these material things. Pursuing them stultifies our spiritual development. The liberation theologians note that one way what they term the oppressors have kept the oppressed under control over the years is to tell them that material things were not important—that the spiritual, especially in a world to come, was what was most important. Yet they themselves did not hesitate to indulge themselves in these material things in the present life. We must realize that if we say, "All that I have is in Jesus," but live as if consumption here is what is most important, the credibility of our testimonies is severely jeopardized.

6. We also must do all that we can to prevent war. Although we have many reasons on other grounds for seeking to combat and prevent war, we are thinking here primarily of the ecological reasons. War always has been destructive of the environment. As the modern technology of war has grown, however, this capacity is greatly multiplied. When Saddam Hussein released a large quantity of oil into the Persian Gulf, the major victims were birds, fish,

and other subhuman organisms. The potential for nuclear war raises the specter of a barren landscape, a nuclear winter, wholesale devastation of life.[8] Christians have a major stake to do all they can to prevent war and should be in the very forefront of efforts to promote peace.

7. We must recognize the rights of other members of the creation besides the humans. All creatures are God's creatures, are objects of His love, and valuable to Him. God placed us on earth not only to utilize these creations for our sake but to manage the universe for the sake of its various inhabitants. We are not the only ones who have divinely bestowed rights.

Of course, a human is more valuable than is a member of another species. Thus, animal rights movements protesting the death of animals through experimentation which makes it possible to spare human lives seriously need to reassess their own value system. Humans' rights take precedence over similar rights of other creatures, but not all rights of humans take precedence over all rights of other creatures. Destroying animal life, not to sustain human life, but merely for human amusement, is not right. Similarly, destroying species of plant life to make human pleasure, comfort, or extravagance possible does not mesh with God's view of the creation.

Here we must accept our responsibility, not merely to enjoy and utilize creation, but to tend, care for and develop it. We must realize that we are the problem. It is not animals and plants that have caused the ecological damage to our universe; it is we. I once heard a theologian say, "If tonight every human being on the earth were to die, tomorrow the entire animal kingdom would rejoice—with the exception of the dog, the Uncle Tom of animals." He was right, of course. For excluding the possibility of conscious awareness of and rejoicing at the death of humans by plants (and animals, for that matter), they would all be better off and would live a better life without us.

Thinking Long Term About the Earth

Two remaining considerations exist about the way in which ethics is done. Long-range concerns must dominate in our thinking and action. This in itself has biblical and theological grounding in the Christian revelation. Jesus, for example, urged his hearers not to lay up for themselves treasures on earth, where they would deteriorate or be stolen, but rather in heaven, where they would not be subject to such dangers (Matt. 6:19-21). Paul wrote that we do not look at the things which are seen, because they are temporary, but at the unseen things, which are eternal (2 Cor. 4:18). James urges us to let perseverance have its complete work (Jas. 1:3-4). We are told that a day is like a thousand years and a thousand years like a day with God (2 Pet. 3:8).

God does not seem to be in a hurry to accomplish His work. Thousands of years elapsed from the Fall to the coming of the Redeemer, and centuries from the giving of the prophecy to its fulfillment. Geology indicates that God apparently did His creative work over what we would deem a long period of time.

The problems we face in ecology have been forming for a long period of time. It should not be surprising if reversing them takes quite some time. We should not seek immediate results or actions whose short-term effects are desirable but whose long-term effects may be very negative.

This does not happen easily within our society. The atmosphere of our time emphasizes immediacy rather than deferral. We see this, for example, in the fact that news reports are live, whereas earlier generations had to wait for hours or even months for reports of some of the most significant events in history. The very structure of society often does not' require deferring of satisfactions.

A very small illustration may make my point. When I was a youth, we listened avidly to radio broadcasts of the stories of our heroes, such as Jack Armstrong (the Wheaties All-American boy) and Tom Mix (of the Tom Mix Ralston Straight Shooters). The radio program offered various types of prizes. These prizes ranged from bandanas to rings which glowed in the dark to decoders enabling the listener to decode secret messages given at the end of the program. In order to receive these special rewards, one had to send in a certain number of box tops from the sponsoring cereal. This took some time, although I was more fortunate than some, since my aunt, as a cook at a senior citizens' residence, could send me box tops by the dozen. Then I would send them in and wait four to six weeks for the prize to come through the mail. I eagerly went to the mailbox each day, beginning with the minimum time. Finally, I received gratification. Today prizes of this type in some cases are still available, but now they are placed within the box! Our ethic will have to go against the trend of this feature of our society, but it will be worth the effort.

Ecological Practices: What Motivates Us

Finally, we need to note the different types of motivation for ethics of ecology. In many cases, these will affect what type of conclusion we draw for our ethical calculation. We will study three types of motivation, in a type of ascending order.

The first is direct self-interest. This is the approach that simply seeks self-satisfaction in terms of pleasure, comfort, recognition, or something else relatively immediate. It often is short-range in nature.

The second is enlightened self-interest. This recognizes that some actions which, on the surface, do not work to one's good and one's comfort, do really accomplish that in the longer run, and some of what seems to be good will in the longer run turn out to be detrimental to oneself. This is the nature of the appeal social ethics often makes. What good does it do to save money by having an automobile without pollution control devices if the resulting condition requires even more severe restrictions and controls at a later point? What good does it do to have lower fuel costs now, if that causes us to fail to develop alternative sources of fuel, so that we become more vulnerable to price fixing by oil suppliers in the future? Some of these may deliberately aim at the welfare of others than oneself, but ultimately that concern is not for the other for the other's sake, but for the sake of oneself. While more sophisticated than crude self-interest, it is not necessarily more unselfish, only more calculating.

The final form of motivation is altruism. Here the appeal is to work for the good of others rather than oneself, whether the other is God, other humans or nonhuman members of the creation. This would show itself in a concern for these others, either simply because they are deemed to have value in themselves, or in the case of the Christian, because of the value God places on them.

We spoke earlier of a sort of ascending order, according to which crass self-interest is the lowest and altruism is the highest. I justify that classification on two grounds. The first is Lawrence Kohlberg's scale of moral development, according to which this sort of progression occurs.[9] The other, however, is biblical and theological. In numerous places, various authors and speakers in the Scripture appeal to altruism. We see it in Paul's appeal to us not to look to our own interests but to the interests of others, as did Jesus (Phil. 2:3-5).

Jesus frequently appealed to His hearers on different levels of motivation. On the one hand, preliminary appeals to nonbelievers may have involved a considerable amount of self-interest. However, he appealed to the more mature listeners to engage in the more self-sacrificial behavior described above (Matt. 16:24-25).

All of this says that a major part of our concern in Christian ethics may be with the person who is the moral actor, or that our ethics will need to be character ethics. Some ethical theories have said that a good act requires four components to be truly good. It must aim at a good end, must utilize a good means, be performed by a good person, and be performed for a good motive. This, however, to the extent that it focuses upon the good person as the moral actor, fits very well with our understanding of the Christian life. Since the general qualities of character, such as humility and unselfishness, are important to us, pursuing them is a major concern for the Christian. Since the major emphasis of evangelical Christianity is transforming persons, God's regenerating and sanctifying grace becomes a major resource for us to accomplish the ethics of ecology.

Notes

1. John W. Klotz, *Ecology Crisis: God's Creation and Man's Pollution* (St. Louis: Concordia, 1971), 5.

2. Joseph Fletcher, *Situation Ethics* (Philadelphia: Westminster, 1966).

3. Christopher Derrick, *The Delicate Creation: Towards a Theology of the Environment* (Old Greenwich, CT: Devin-Adair, 1972), 78.

4. Ron Elsdon, *Bent World: A Christian Response to the Environmental Crisis* (Downers Grove: InterVarsity, 1981), 140-41.

5. May Evelyn Jegen, "The Church's Role in Healing the Earth," *Tending the Garden: Essays on the Gospel and the Earth*, ed. Wesley Granberg-Michaelson (Grand Rapids: Eerdmans, 1987), 103.

6. Elsdon, *Bent World*, 123.

7. Ibid., 4-5.

8. Wesley Granberg-Michaelson, *A Worldly Spirituality: The Call to Redeem Life on Earth* (San Francisco: Harper and Row, 1984), 3.

9. Lawrence Kohlberg, *The Psychology of Moral Development: Moral Stages and the Life Cycle* (San Francisco: Harper and Row, 1984).

6

The New Age Movement and the Environment

Gary H. Leazer

To many people the New Age movement is a mass of sensational practices and confusing and contradictory beliefs. Christians are certain these practices and beliefs are fundamentally hostile to basic Christian doctrines, but they are hard pressed to explain those differences thoroughly.

With its fuzzy parameters and non-Christian world view, the New Age movement is difficult, but not impossible, to understand. The New Age movement is more than channeling and crystals, its two most sensational aspects. It is a pervasive alternative religious movement having as its goal to change radically every aspect of life on this planet. Of two things this writer is certain: The New Age movement probably is the most serious challenge to the Christian faith today, and no Christian is immune from exposure to New Age influence.

We generally may define the New Age movement as an informal, loosely organized, and complex network of hundreds of groups and individuals holding a common world view, value system, and vision concerning humankind's religious, economic, health care, educational, environmental, social, and political life. The New Age movement began to appear in the United States in the late 1960s, but New Age ideas have existed for hundreds of years.

We see the diversity of the New Age movement in its attempt to combine several types of meditation, positive thinking, faith healing, rolfing, dietary reform, environmentalism, mysticism, yoga, acupuncture, incense, astrology, biofeedback, extrasensory perception, evolution, nature religions, Sufism, chiropractic, herbal medicine, hypnosis, elements from major world religions, and any other technique to heighten awareness.[1]

We find this diversity in nearly every area of life. New Age themes are in various kinds of entertainment from movies and television "talk shows" to music. Many popular entertainers are well-known people in New Age circles. Actor Dennis Weaver regularly leads workshops at New Age seminars and fairs. Singer John Denver's Windstar Foundation has as its goal calling forth a "spirit of transformation" related to ecological concerns and planetary consciousness. Ecological events and issues, such as Earth Day and concern about the destruction of the world's rain forests, attract widespread New Age interest.

Business seminars claiming to improve employee morale or productivity can be New Age. Alternative medicine and healing methods and products can be New Age. New Age newspapers, magazines, and books appear in abundance in thousands of bookstores. New Age bookstores often are places where New Age teachers offer public seminars. New Age expositions and fairs often bring hundreds of people together for a potpourri of New Age practices, techniques, and lectures. Retreat centers and communes, computer bulletin boards, and New Age curriculum for public schools introduce thousands of others to the New Age philosophy.

Not every religious group opposed to biblical and historic Christianity is New Age. Neither the Unification Church nor the Baha'i World Faith, both of which teach that the Christian era has ended, is New Age. Their teachings are too exclusive for the New Age movement. Each has a particular founder and a specific set of doctrines to which followers are expected to adhere.

Historical and Spiritual Roots

The New Age movement is not a single group in one location. One can find New Age groups in hundreds of locations across the United States. Although individuals such as Marilyn Ferguson,

David Spangler, and Barbara Marx Hubbard are popular New Age teachers, no single leader or teacher is accepted by all New Agers.

While the teachings and practices of the New Age movement are diverse, we can trace its spiritual roots to several other movements, groups, and individuals. The three distinct foundations of the New Age movement are the occult world, Asian world religions, and the optimistic human potential movement of the 1960s. Although stressed by a number of New Age teachers, including Benjamin Creme of the Tara Center, Christianity and the Bible play only a minor part in New Age philosophy. As we will see, when New Agers cite Christianity and the Bible, they reject basic Christian doctrines concerning the personality of God, uniqueness of Jesus Christ, sin, and judgment. Hinduism and other Asian religious and philosophical concepts form the major religious foundation of the New Age movement. Hinduism first was popularized in the United States by American Transcendentalists (1835-1860), such as Ralph Waldo Emerson, who borrowed from the Hindu *Bhagavad Gita* and wrote of God as the Great Oversoul within nature and every person.

The New Thought movement of the last half of the nineteenth century is a forerunner of the New Age movement. The New Thought movement attempted to appear Christian, but its theological foundation most clearly is seen in Hinduism. The Unity School of Christianity, the Church of Religious Science, and the Church of Christ Scientist are present-day expressions of the New Thought movement. Ministers and members of the Unity School of Christianity often are personally involved in the New Age movement. New Age books often cite Unity publications. Unity bookstores regularly carry a wide variety of New Age books.

Gnostic influence is apparent in New Age thought, as many New Age teachers acknowledge. Gnostism, condemned as heretical by the early church, argues that a person will receive enlightenment or realization of his or her divine nature through knowledge of secret teachings and practices available to select individuals.

Channeling is the best-known Gnostic practice within the New Age movement as individuals claim to receive knowledge long lost to humankind. The source of this knowledge is said to be historical and nonhistorical persons and entities from such places as Atlantis and outer space.

Theosophy, founded by Helena Blavatsky (1831-1891) in 1875, has done more than any other group to popularize Hindu ideas in America. Theosophy also is a Gnostic system with its emphasis on "secret doctrines" revealed by "ascended masters." We can trace the roots of many New Age teachings directly to ideas promoted by Theosophy.[2]

We also can trace roots of the New Age movement to the Arcane School Alice Bailey founded in 1923 after she left the Theosophical Society. People credit Bailey with first using the name "New Age." The Arcane School has influenced many New Age teachers including Benjamin Creme. Creme is best known for his full-page newspaper advertisements announcing "The Christ is Now Here" in 1982.

The human potential movement, the Age of Aquarius, the occult revival, and the influx of Eastern religions into the United States in the 1960s helped create an atmosphere which gave birth to the New Age movement. The human potential movement was popular with its teaching that human beings have unlimited power to determine their own destiny, making humans equal in power with God. The Age of Aquarius stargazers claimed that as the earth moved into the new Age of Aquarius, the Christian era, seen as being identical with the Age of Pisces, ended. The occult revival created again an interest in nature, magic, spiritualism, UFOs, and stories of lost civilizations.

People often confuse the New Age movement with secular humanism. The New Age movement and secular humanism agree at a number of significant points: their approach to ethics, their interest in solving social problems, their aversion to dogmatic religion, their interest in using science and technology to change the world, their interest with alternative sources of knowledge, and their interest in the future. However, the New Age movement is a spiritual system; it assumes a spiritual reality. Secular humanism denies that life has a spiritual dimension; it rejects the belief in God, revelation or life after death. While the New Age movement appeals to many secularly oriented people because of its nontraditional, noninstitutional, and noncreedal ideas, we should understand it as religious or cosmic humanism, not secular humanism.[3]

The New Age World View

Several unifying characteristics are inherent in the New Age world view.

1. The first assumption of the New Age world view is that "all is one." By this is meant that the cosmos and everything that exists is of one and the same essence or reality. New Agers often use impersonal terms such as "life force," Mind, Power, Energy, Being, Awareness, or Consciousness to describe this so-called monistic reality.

This monistic view stands in stark contrast to the biblical affirmation of a personal, spiritual power behind and beyond the material universe. The Bible affirms that God created the universe out of nothingness (*ex nihilo*) at some specific point in time and continues to sustain its existence.[4] A clear understanding of the biblical doctrine of creation is essential for a proper understanding of our role as stewards of the earth and its resources.

2. The second assumption closely follows; namely, that "all is god." Jane Roberts, who claimed to channel an entity called Seth, referred to God as "All That Is."[5] The theological term describing this position is pantheism. We can trace this position to monistic Hinduism, which holds that the Oversoul merely expanded "itself" to become the universe. A pantheist holds that ultimately no difference exists between God, a person, a tree, or earth. As early as 1972, historian Arnold Toynbee placed the worldwide ecological problems at the feet of the Judeo-Christian religion and specifically cited Genesis 1:28 as the biblical sanction to exploit the earth and its resources. He advised returning to the pantheistic world view of the pre-Judeo-Christian era.[6]

Persons who call themselves Pagans, Neo-Pagans, Witches, or Wiccans also hold a pantheistic view of God. While not a part of the New Age movement in its most strict definition, Pagan or occult groups and the New Age movement hold similar world views and goals concerning humankind and the environment. People often say paganism is an ecological religion because of its reverence for the earth and nature. One occult group, Feraferia, has as its purpose "to save the earth and return humanity to a state of harmony with nature."[7] We must make one important distinction between Paganism and the New Age movement. While both are pantheistic, Paganism accepts the idea of polytheism, while the New Age movement is monistic.

New Age leaders cite the Gaia Hypothesis when they discuss the teaching termed planetary consciousness. People define planetary consciousness as a world view which places loyalties to all living beings, including the earth, above loyalties to self, individual people, groups, or nations. The Gaia Hypothesis proposes that the earth and all life upon it form one living being.

The Gaia Hypothesis appears to have been developed by two individuals in the early 1970s. Otter G'Zel (born Tim Zell), founder of the Neo-Pagan organization Church of All Worlds, claims to have had a vision in 1970 that the biosphere was a single living organization. All life, G'Zell argued in *The Green Egg*, his church's magazine, evolved from a single cell and carries with it the life of that original cell.[8]

At about the same time, James Lovelock, an atmospheric biochemist, came to a similar conclusion that the earth was a single living organism. Lovelock called his theory the Gaia Hypothesis after the Greek Mother Goddess Gaia. Lovelock sees Gaia as more than the sum of all living organisms, just as human life is more than the sum of all a body's cells. All life forms part of Gaia, but they are not synonymous. Lovelock argues that the earth is a self-organizing and self-regulating entity with the capacity to keep itself healthy by controlling the chemical and physical environment.[9] He says the earth always keeps itself fit for life. Any species, including humankind, which violates her rules, for example by polluting the environment, will be destroyed.

The New Age movement has given the Gaia Hypothesis a place of immense importance. Not only has the Gaia Hypothesis become the religious foundation for environmental concerns but also for attitudes and policies toward animal rights. People use it in debates concerning animal experimentation for developing new drugs or cosmetics, capturing dolphins in tuna nets, and killing whales and baby seals. The Findhorn Community in Scotland is an example of a New Age community living out the Gaia Hypothesis. Some New Age groups have taken the name, such as The Gaia Institute in Atlanta, Georgia, and offer programs for planetary renewal.[10]

The Bible, on the other hand, affirms that not all is God. Rather, God the Creator is distinct from His creation; He created the universe out of nothing, not out of Himself (Gen. 1:1, Mark 10:6). The biblical position stands in stark contrast with the pantheism of the New Age movement. Biblical creation and pantheism are diametrically opposed to each other. The earth does not have a life of its own; the sustaining power of a caring God sustains it.

3. The third assumption naturally follows from the first two: Since all is one and all is god, then humanity is inherently divine. In other words, the true Self is divine. The goal of all New Age techniques is to change the thinking of humans so they will know they are divine. Barbara Marx Hubbard, writing the foreword in Alan Cohen's *The Healing of the Planet Earth*, says humankind must take a "quantum leap" to realize it is "a co-creative human, who is one with the Source of creation. . . . We are God-in-expression."[11]

The Bible clearly states that God created humans in His own image (Gen. 1:27). To be created in the image of God means that in many respects we are like God,[12] but we are not a part or spark of God. Human beings have intelligence, can reason, are aware of their existence, have freedom of choice, and can respond to God's initiative because they are created in God's image. While humans are a part of God's creation, they are unique in His creation. No other creature enjoys this special relationship with God. This truth not only tells us about ourselves but also something about the nature of God. He is personal. He is able to respond to our prayers, which the pantheistic god of the New Age movement is unable to do.

The New Age movement gives Jesus a place, but the New Age understanding of Jesus is not that of the Bible. Elizabeth Clare Prophet, leader of the Church Universal and Triumphant in Livingston, Montana, claims Jesus is an "ascended master" who during his so-called silent years traveled to India to study Hinduism. Prophet claims she has channeled Jesus and learned that His actual teachings were removed from the Bible by early Christians. Her books present Jesus as a man who discovered His divinity, the same divinity hidden within every person. She rejects the uniqueness of Jesus as Savior and Lord.

Benjamin Creme placed full-page advertisements in a number of major newspapers in 1982 announcing that "The Christ is Now Here." According to the ad, Creme's Christ is the "World Teacher, Lord Maitreya," known not only as Jesus of Nazareth, but also as Krishna, the fifth Buddha, and Iman Mahdi. *The Urantia Book*, a 2,097-page volume first published in 1955, allegedly was channeled from various beings. It claims, among other things, to be a history of earth, called Urantia, using the biblical story. Jesus is said to have been born August 21, 7 B.C., to have received an excellent education, and to have traveled throughout the Mediterranean area. His three-year public ministry ended with His crucifixion in A.D. 27.

The Fifth Epochal Fellowship, formerly the Urantia Brotherhood, promotes *The Urantia Book* as containing the true teachings of Jesus.[13] Other New Age teachers claim Jesus did not die on the cross but survived the ordeal and traveled again to India where He died.[14] We cannot reconcile any of these or other New Age views of Jesus with the biblical revelation.

More New Age Teachings

4. Fourth, humankind's basic problem is its ignorance of the oneness of all and consequently of its own divinity. A belief in karma and reincarnation are attendant doctrines of this position. Because humans are divine, they do really die but also live successive lives until they have attained God-consciousness or Self-consciousness or enlightenment about their true nature. They have unlimited potential. They are limited only because of their ignorance of their divinity, but ignorance can be eliminated by numerous techniques. New Agers see the human problem as ignorance, a sort of spiritual amnesia, rather than a willful, sinful rebellion against a loving, personal God. Humankind is basically good. That humankind has rebelled against a moral God is foreign to the New Age movement, since the movement holds that the human being is his own god and has complete control over his future. Not only is relativism seen in New Age teachings concerning the solution to humankind's problem but also in an individual's ethical relationships to others. Each person must choose a personal moral standard. "Create your own reality" is a common New Age phrase. People must decide for themselves what they believe.

The Bible is very clear concerning humankind's basic problem. It is willful rebellion against a holy God. This rebellion has brought sin to all humankind (Rom. 3:23, 5:12). Rather than having unlimited power to determine the future, humankind is powerless to rescue itself from the bonds of sin. Because of this hopeless situation, God in His infinite mercy took the initiative to bring His grace to every person who will receive it (Rom. 5:1-11).

5. Fifth, the New Age teaches that all people can change their thinking, transform their own consciousness, realize their own divinity, and create their own reality. People can accomplish this through such New Age techniques as meditation, chanting, wearing crystals, biofeedback, dream interpretation, channeling, hypnosis, guided imagery, visualization, and following special diets.

Other ways are using alternative healing techniques such as rolfing, iridology, full-body herbal wraps, reflexology, chiropractic, and massages. Still other ways involve numerous occult and Asian philosophies such as Tai-Chi, yoga, astrology, past life regression, Shamanism, and almost any other mystic or psychic experience to alter a person's former perception of reality. The three-volume *Course in Miracles*, allegedly channeled by Helen Schucman in 1965-1972 from an entity who claimed to be Jesus, is one of the most popular New Age courses; it claims to be an alternative, but unorthodox, approach to Christianity.[15] According to the New Age, a person is his or her own savior.

The Bible teaches that a person cannot save self. Humanity does not receive God's forgiveness through any technique but rather as a free gift available to any person by grace through faith (Eph. 2:8-10). While the Bible speaks of being "transformed by the renewing of your mind," it is apparent that this occurs only by the mercies and grace of God (Rom. 12:1-3).

6. Sixth, personal transformation must precede global transformation. While differing on how this will occur, all New Agers believe the human race is on the verge of a time of mass self-enlightenment which will bring solutions to worldwide problems concerning the environment, poverty, crime, racism, international relations, diseases, etc. Some New Agers speak of one world language, one monetary system, one world government and, of course, one world religion.

Marilyn Ferguson, author of the half-million copy best-seller *The Aquarian Conspiracy*, argues that personal transformation can lead to collective and then to global transformation.[16] She claims a "quantum leap" soon will suddenly bring a higher form of life as the human race realizes its oneness and divinity.[17]

This is the theory behind the New Age event, Harmonic Convergence. Harmonic Convergence is an event when particularly powerful cosmic forces allegedly cause a collective shift in human consciousness. This shift is said to influence the entire planet.

Mexican-born art historian Jose Arguelles argued in his 1975 book, *The Transformative Vision*, that humankind had forgotten its relationship to the earth as a living organism. Arguelles argued that this would change with what he called a "climax of matter."

Using the Mayan calendar, Arguelles calculated that a period of nine 52-year cycles, beginning with the arrival of Cortes in Central America, had their climax in 1987. These cycles allegedly occur within a large cosmic cycle of 5,125 years, which runs from 3113 B.C. to A.D. 2012. According to Arguelles, a climax occurred on August 16-17, 1987, at which time the earth entered a new period of purification and cleansing, which will climax again with the true Harmonic Convergence in A.D. 2012.

Arguelles believes the result of the Harmonic Convergence will be that all military weapons will be eliminated, environmental pollution will end, and heightened human potential including parapsychological abilities will emerge.

Arguelles' theory became popular after an article about it appeared in the June 23, 1987, issue of the *Wall Street Journal*. The theory received additional publicity in the July 27, 1987, issue of *Newsweek* featuring Shirley MacLaine on the cover. As a result, a number of New Age groups made plans for the first Harmonic Convergence on August 16-17. New Age followers gathered at 350 "sacred sites" from California's Mount Shasta to the Great Pyramids of Egypt to Stonehenge in England to bring peace and harmony to the earth. Although organizers set a worldwide goal of 144,000, attendance fell far short of the goal, with actual attendance estimates of 20,000 "rainbow humans."[18]

The 1987 Harmonic Convergence was met with ridicule. A "Doonesbury" cartoon called it "moronic convergence . . . sort of a national fruit loops day."[19] Archaeologists quickly said they could find no confirmation of Arguelles' theories in their study of the Mayan calendar.[20] Although several groups have attempted to continue the Harmonic Convergence idea, it has been met with limited enthusiasm.

We find an idea similar to Harmonic Convergence, where a specific number of persons collectively meditating together allegedly can change reality, in the so-called Hundredth Monkey Myth. We can trace the myth of the hundredth monkey to a 1953 study of a group of macaque monkeys on the Japanese island of Koshima. Lyall Watson devoted two pages about the study in his 1979 book, *Lifetide: A Biology of the Unconscious.* New Age writers soon cited his account to support their theory that when enough people adopt a new idea, it will change the consciousness of all humankind.

According to Watson, scientists left sweet potatoes for the monkeys to better observe their behavior. One of the monkeys began washing the sand and dirt off the potatoes in the ocean before she ate the potatoes. She soon taught this behavior to others in her troop.

The Hundredth Monkey Myth assumes that at a certain threshold or "critical mass," usually said to have occurred when the hundredth monkey began washing potatoes, the behavior became a universal practice. This practice is said to have occurred not only within the group of monkeys on this particular part of Koshima but across natural barriers on the island and on other islands.

The story became popular among New Age followers, especially after Ken Keyes, Jr., wrote the best-seller, *The Hundredth Monkey,* in 1982.[21] After this book and several articles in quasi-scientific journals were published, people accepted the myth as if it were scientific.

While New Agers such as Keyes accept Watson's brief account as scientific evidence, it is not clear that Watson really was certain of his account. He admits he gathered the story from "personal anecdotes and bits of folklore" because the scientists were not quite certain what really occurred on Koshima.[22]

The idea that universal spiritual change can occur when a specific number of believers wills it is not unique to the New Age movement. Transcendental Meditation guru Maharishi Mahesh Yogi inaugurated "The Dawn of the Age of Enlightenment" in 1975, predicting the beginning of a new period of human history which would see the end of all human suffering and tragedy. Maharishi argues that group meditation has a greater effect on the world than the same number of persons meditating separately. He claims that if the square root of one percent of the world's population, or 7,000 people, would meditate collectively, the world would move toward the Age of Enlightenment.[23]

Christians accept their responsibility for the world because it is God's creation (Ps. 24:1) and because God has given humankind responsibility for the stewardship of His creation (Gen. 1:26; 2:15). Because sin has invaded the entire creation, Christians also look to the Second Coming when God in Christ will return to renew the earth (Rom. 8:19-21; Rev. 21:1).

7. Seventh, the New Age movement argues that all religions are true and, therefore, ultimately one. In other words, it makes no difference which religious teacher or path a person takes, for no one way is any better than another. No one religion has all truth; many truths exist, New Agers claim. New Age teachers such as Shirley MacLaine often speak of these as "realities."[24]

The Bible presents Jesus as the unique Lord and Savior of the world. Who Jesus is, what He taught, and what He has done for humankind makes Him unique among all religious teachers. He is the heart of Christianity. Because He is unique, Christianity is unique. He is not one among many; He is incomparable (Col. 1:15-22).

The New Age Movement and Planetary Consciousness

Planetary consciousness, defined earlier as the New Age term for a world view which places loyalties to all living beings, including the earth, above loyalties to self, individual people, groups, or nations, is one of the driving forces behind New Age practices. Planetary consciousness has developed in a number of directions.

Communes have inspired numerous New Age members by providing opportunities to incorporate the New Age world view into everyday life. Communes are generally intentional, that is, organized for some ideological purpose such as some global crisis.

Communes provide a clear alternative to materialistic individualism and the resulting destruction of the environment, both of which are primary New Age concerns. Besides offering an opportunity for understanding the reality of the interdependence of all life, they provide models for creative change in the larger society. Only by finding ways to transform self within the context of a small group, do communards, or persons living in communes, believe ways can be discovered to transform the larger society. Communards see themselves as forerunners of a new society through experimenting with new approaches to problems of over-population, pollution, limited natural resources, and divisions among nations and people groups. Sharing possessions, work, and space brings a sense of unity and oneness in the community, which it is hoped can spread to all humankind.

Communes, some of which prefer to be called "eco-villages," have a strong emphasis on "living lightly on the earth," which means reducing consumption, recycling resources, and using renewable sources of energy such as wood, solar, and wind. A dedication to healing the earth and working in harmony with the forces of nature are foundational goals of New Age communes.[25]

Two types of communes exist. The first is older communes which are sympathetic with New Age philosophy, goals, and ideals. Many were founded in the 1960s and 1970s as religious, primarily Hindu, Buddhist or Sufi, communes. The Abode of the Message is a 450-acre Sufi commune, established in 1974, in New Lebanon, New York. Sixty adults and 25 children are permanent residents.[26] One hundred adults and children live on the 700-acre Ananda Cooperative Village, begun by disciples of Swami Yogananda, in Nevada City, California.[27] These communes, and dozens of others, provide seminars on meditation, vegetarianism, and environmental issues. The second type of commune is those which were founded as New Age communities. The Findhorn Community in Scotland and Auroville, an 11,000-acre cooperative in India, are the two most prominent communes founded as New Age communities. The 240-acre Stelle community, located near Kankakee,

Illinois, is one of the most prominent of the dozens of New Age communes scattered across the United States.[28]

The Findhorn Community in northern rural Scotland perhaps is the most important New Age commune. It was founded in 1965 by Eileen Caddy, Peter Caddy, and Dorothy Maclean. American-born David Spangler served as education director at Findhorn from 1970 to 1973 before leaving to form his own New Age group, the Lorian Association, in Belmont, California.[29] The Lorian Association moved to Middleton, Wisconsin, around 1980 and then to Issaquah, Washington, at the end of the decade. Lorian Association members commit themselves to harmless interaction with the environment, conservation, the wise use of energy, and the building of a planetary village.[30]

Channeling has been an important part of Findhorn teaching since the earliest days. Findhorn's teaching in this area is directed toward forces or spirits in nature. Findhorn members seek attunement or "at-one-ment" with "devas" in nature. "Deva" is a Sanskrit word meaning spirit. Devas are believed to be guiding forces which give structure and energy to the plant world. Communication with devas is said to be possible. Findhorn members are responsible for nurturing the devas by realizing that "they, like the kingdom of heaven, are within us."[31] Thus, at Findhorn, members attempt to find harmony and a oneness of life with the community and all of nature.

This emphasis on the interdependency of life is believed to provide physical, mental, and emotional healing energy, both for the individual and the earth. As members learn how to be responsible for their gardens, they begin to feel responsible for the whole planet.

A belief in the interdependence and interconnectedness of all life also was the reason behind the creation of Auroville. A "model" of human unity and planetary consciousness, Auroville has suffered a number of serious internal problems almost since its beginning in 1968.[32]

Proponents practice vegetarianism because of concern for planetary consciousness. Some practice vegetarianism because of the amount of land and grain needed to produce the meat; others because they do not wish to be party to inflicting pain on an animal as it is killed for its meat. Others practice it because they believe meat products, and even chemically produced grains and processed food, may hinder the pursuit of enlightenment. Vegetarian advocates also say their lifestyle reduces over-grazing by animals which can lead to soil erosion and increase the trend toward desert-like conditions.

While vegetarianism is an important theme in the New Age movement, vegetarianism far predates its arrival. Seventh-day Adventist John Harvey Kellogg and his brother Will Keith Kellogg, who developed a cereal company bearing their name, were early vegetarians. The New Age movement follows vegetarianism with a variety of degrees. Many abstain from meat products (beef, pork, fish, and chicken) but consume animal products such as milk, cheese, eggs, and honey. Others refrain from the use of all animal products, even refusing to wear leather, wool, or decorative feathers. Others advocate a diet of primarily cereal, or raw foods, or fruits.[33] More than 6,000 natural food stores in the United States reported sales totaling $3.3 billion in 1987.[34]

Barbara Marx Hubbard has been a major spokesperson for planetary consciousness for two decades. She is the co-founder of the Foundation for Co-Creation and the Institute for the Study of Conscious Evolution. She is the author of several books and is a frequent writer in New Age magazines.[35]

Norman Cousins, publisher of the *Saturday Review*, Donald Keyes, and former United Nations secretary general U Thant formed Planetary Citizens, an organization dedicated to addressing a variety of concerns, including ecology.[36]

A "night club with conscience" in Manhattan is dedicated "to raising consciousness on environmental issues." The Wetlands Preserve exposes patrons to a myriad of environmental and social issues with flyers, posters, and a calendar of upcoming programs at the club.[37]

Wisconsin Senator Gaylord Nelson is credited by the New Age movement for suggesting a day for Americans to focus on serious environmental problems.[38] Environmentalists, such as Barry Commoner, organized what has become known as Earth Day on April 22, 1970. The event addressed a wide variety of environmental concerns, primarily by students on college and university campuses. Acid rain, the use of hydrocarbons, overpopulation, and hunger were among those concerns. Students on a Florida campus held a trial to condemn a car for polluting the air and then tried to "execute" it with sledgehammers. Students at another campus staged an "Earth service" of Sanskrit incantations. Earth Day has been observed sporadically on local levels since 1970, mostly by persons holding a New Age world view.

In the late 1970s, Marxist and other far-left activists joined to establish the Green Party in West Germany. Although known for its anti-war policy, the Green Party attracted most of its support because of its stand on the environment. In the early 1980s, the Green Party spread to the United States. Its strategy in this country includes tracking candidates' positions and voting records on environmental issues. A Green movement conference in Massachusetts in July 1987 attracted 1,500 people from over 37 states and nine countries.[39] The Greens say they have organized in about 250 communities in the United States. The core group in Atlanta numbers approximately 40 persons.[40]

The media also helps spread New Age planetary consciousness. In February 1991, the Turner Broadcasting System broadcast a five-night program entitled "Voice of the Planet." Starring William Shatner, playing an ecologist-author, and Faye Dunaway, playing the earth spirit Gaia, the program's basic message was, "Wake up, humanity, you're killing the planet."[41]

New Age movement investment firms encourage ethical investing, by which they mean investing in companies which are socially aware of their responsibility to planetary consciousness. For example, they recommend companies that have demonstrated a concern for society and the environment, and welfare and safety of their employees and consumers. They avoid buy-recommendations for industries with military, nuclear, or chemical fertilizer contracts because these products are seen as destructive to the environment.

They promote recycling to conserve energy, as it takes less energy to recycle an item than to produce it, to protect natural resources, to reduce dependence on foreign energy, to reduce the need for coal and oil-fueled power plants, and to slow the need for new landfills.

New Age magazines and New Age fairs promote alternative forms of transportation to reduce air pollution emitted from automobiles. The concern about global warming has found a receptive ear with New Age followers. The rapid depletion of tropical rain forests in South America, Africa, and parts of southeast Asia affects rainfall and other weather conditions over much of the earth. New Age followers are concerned about the destruction of rain forests because they are home to thousands of plants, animals, birds and insects found nowhere else. They are quick to say that natural drugs to fight many diseases can be found in the plants being destroyed as the rain forests are destroyed.

New Age books and magazines list literally hundreds of practical suggestions to protect the environment.[42] They include composting organic materials, keeping a bottle of cold water in the refrigerator to save tap water lost in order to get cool water, refusing to use products with nonbiodegradable or nonrecyclable packing, refusing to use disposable diapers, planting trees, and hundreds of other activities following the New Age motto: "thinking globally, but acting locally."

Responding to the New Age Challenge

Christians need to understand what the New Age movement is and is not. It is easy to succumb to paranoia and to find the New Age movement behind every bush and in everything with which we personally disagree. Marilyn Ferguson's book, *The Aquarian Conspiracy*, has led some Christians to draw unsubstantiated conclusions about the New Age movement. Her book is her optimistic dream about the future, but this writer and many other evangelical scholars can find no evidence of a measurable New Age conspiracy at this time.[43] It is this writer's measured conclusion that Ferguson's dream will come true only if Christians fail to rise to meet this growing and serious challenge. The New Age movement will move in wherever and whenever the Christian church fails to fulfill its biblical mandate and leaves a void in society.

Christians desperately need to more effectively integrate their faith into everyday life and issues. For example, Christians need to develop practical methods of implementing the Christian doctrine of the stewardship of God's creation in specific ways in society. New Age followers put many Christians to shame by their willingness to become personally involved in efforts to protect the environment. They desire to protect the earth because they believe the earth is divine. Christians should protect the earth because it is God's creation. Christians must not only preach the gospel but also be the "salt of the earth" and "light of the world" (Matt. 5:13-14, KJV).

Christians must be careful they do not reinforce New Age followers' misconceptions about evangelical Christianity as being out of touch with twentieth-century life and Christians as ignorant about issues facing humankind. Sensational reporting of New Age beliefs and practices without solid documentation always is counterproductive. In many ways, the New Age movement is more a product of the media than of its own historical and spiritual roots. The media, always looking for the sensational and spectacular, found both in such New Age practices as channeling and crystals. Without this publicity, this writer believes the New Age movement would have passed from center stage much as has the human potential movement since the 1960s.

Christians must be careful they do not allow certain buzzwords to become their favorite fears. Words like peace, holistic, global, rainbow, and transformation do not always reflect New Age thinking. While the New Age movement is anti-Christ because it replaces Jesus Christ with another savior—namely, humankind itself, this conclusion creates more heat than light.

Christians need to realize that most New Age followers are genuinely sincere. They do not perceive their beliefs and practices as irrational or inconsistent. Christians need to expose New Age teachings and practices wherever they are found and then show a "more excellent way" (1 Cor. 12:31, KJV). Christians need to admit that in at least one sense the New Age movement is not all bad, for it reminds us that people have spiritual needs and desires.

In response to the New Age challenge, Christians must positively and effectively present the gospel to New Age followers. Walter Martin calls for a two-pronged approach in responding to the New Age challenge: "maximum exposure and penetration of Christian evangelism and apologetics."[44] We must produce Christian literature which will effectively communicate the gospel to New Age followers who have not considered, have rejected, or are hostile to the Christian church.

Much of our evangelistic material and methods are directed at persons who accept the Judeo-Christian world view. Christians must produce evangelistic material which speaks directly to New Age concerns and world view. One excellent source is a New Testament, entitled *Born to Be Reborn,* available from the World Home Bible League in South Holland, Illinois. This edition of the New Testament contains inserts with questions and statements that New Age followers are asking or making and then gives appropriate biblical responses.

The Bible charges us as Christians to be faithful witnesses of the gospel by word and deed. New Age followers desperately seek some good news about life, the world, and their future. We have that Good News and have been charged by the Creator of all things to share it with everyone who asks us to give an account of the hope we have, "yet with gentleness and reverence" (1 Pet. 3:15, NASB).

Notes

1. Christopher Lasch, "Soul of a New Age," *Omni* (October, 1987), 81.

2. Maurice Smith, "A Christian Perspective on the New Age Movements," *Search* (Winter, 1990), 12-19.

3. See Douglas R. Groothuis, *Unmasking the New Age* (Downers Grove: InterVarsity, 1986), 167 and Philip H. Lochhaas, *How to Respond to The New Age Movement* (St. Louis: Concordia, 1988), 14-15 for a clear presentation of the differences between secular humanism and the New Age movement.

4. Roy T. Edgemon, *The Doctrines Baptists Believe* (Nashville: Convention, 1988), 30-33.

5. Jane Roberts, *Dreams, "Evolution," and Value Fulfillment*, Volume 1 (New York: Prentice Hall, 1986), 132.

6. Margot Adler, *Drawing Down the Moon* (Boston: Beacon, 1986), 17-18.

7. Ibid., 251.

8. J. Gordon Melton, *New Age Encyclopedia* (Detroit: Gale, 1990), 183.

9. James E. Lovelock, *Gaia: A New Look at Life on Earth* (New York: Oxford University Press, 1979), p. xii; see also James E. Lovelock, *The Ages of Gaia* (New York: Norton, 1988), 31.

10. *Thought Trends* (February, 1991), 19.

11. Alan Cohen, *The Healing of the Planet Earth: Personal Power and Planetary Transformation* (Atlanta: New Leaf, 1987), p. vii.

12. Edgemon, 36.

13. J. Gordon Melton, *The Encyclopedia of American Religions*, Second Edition (Detroit: Gale, 1987), 590.

14. Douglas Groothuis, *Revealing the New Age Jesus: Challenges to Orthodox Views of Christ* (Downers Grove: InterVarsity, 1990), 166.

15. *A Course in Miracles* (New York: Foundation for Inner Peace, 1975).

16. Marilyn Ferguson, *The Aquarian Conspiracy: Personal and Social Transformation in our Time* (Los Angeles: Tarcher, 1980), 411.

17. Ibid., 156-57.

18. Melton, *New Age Encyclopedia*, 204-05 and Russell Chandler, *Understanding the New Age* (Dallas: Word, 1988), 96-100.

19. Chandler, 97.

20. Melton, *New Age Encyclopedia*, 205.

21. Ken Keyes, Jr., *The Hundredth Monkey* (Coos Bay, OR: Vision, 1982).

22. Melton, *New Age Encyclopedia*, 226.

23. "Are the Maharishi's 7,000 meditators ready to fly?" *Des Moines Register*, December 21, 1983; "Utopia Thinking in Iowa," *Newsweek*, January 2, 1984, 31; *Age of Enlightenment News* (Fairfield, Iowa: Maharishi International University, 1984), 3.

24. Douglas Groothuis, "A Transformed Shirley MacLaine?" *SCP Newsletter* (September-October, 1983), 11-12.

25. Corinne McLaughlin and Gordon Davidson, *Builders of the Dawn: Community Lifestyles in a Changing World* (Shutesbury, MA: Sirius, 1986), 22-23.

26. Ibid., 350.

27. Ibid.

28. Ibid., 360.

29. Melton, *New Age Encyclopedia*, 428-29.

30. Ibid., 268.

31. McLaughlin and Davidson, 239.

32. Melton, *New Age Encyclopedia*, 50-52.

33. Ibid., 14, 484-87.

34. *The 1988 Guide to New Age Living* (Winter, 1988), 6.

35. Melton, *New Age Encyclopedia*, 223.

36. Ibid., 357.

37. Rochel Haigh Blehr, "New York City Bar Serves Up Drinks, Dancing and Desire to Save Earth," *Alternatives for a New Age* (January, 1990), 1.

38. Donna Campbell, "Earth Day Spans Two Decades of Activism," *Alternatives for a New Age* (April, 1990), 1-3.

39. *The 1988 Guide to New Age Living* (Winter, 1988), 6.

40. Lynn Edwards, "The Greens and America's Grass Roots," *Alternatives for a New Age* (July 1990), 4.

41. *The Atlanta Journal/The Atlanta Constitution*, February 18, 1991.

42. One source is Jeremy Rifkin, *The Green Lifestyle Handbook: 1001 Ways You Can Heal the Earth* (New York: Henry Holt and Co., 1990).

43. Elliott Miller, who is editor of the *Christian Research Journal*, has written an excellent critique of the conspiracy theory popular among several Christian writers in his book, *A Crash Course on the New Age Movement* (Grand Rapids: Baker, 1989), 193-206. The *Christian Research Journal* is published by the late Walter Martin's Christian Research Institute.

44. Walter Martin, *The New Age Cult* (Minneapolis: Bethany, 1989), 97-101.

7

The Environment, Ethics, and Exposition

David S. Dockery

Christianity often has been used as the scapegoat for the environmental crisis. Whether this actually is the case, churches have offered mixed signals and responses to current issues about the environment. Rarely does one hear a sermon on such matters, especially in churches committed to faithful biblical exposition. This chapter addresses the issues related to environmental concerns from a theological and ethical perspective.

The purpose of this examination is to point us in the direction of exposition. We want to see how we can relate the biblical witness to these matters. Or, to put it another way: In addressing environmental concerns, how do we move from text to ethics to exposition?

Developing a Biblical Ethic

The problem with trying to speak about the ethics of the Bible is that ethical contents are not offered apart from the doctrinal teaching of the Bible. Thus, to answer questions such as: "What is meant by good?" "Who is good?" "How ought we to behave so as to do the good?" requires us first to look at God. We must see what God is in His character and what He wills in His revelation, for this defines what is good, right, and ethical.

Unfortunately, in many circles Christian ethics has developed into its own discipline and has become separated from biblical exegesis and theology. Where it has remained in touch with the biblical message, some have seriously questioned whether a unified ethical teaching can be found. They believe too much diversity exists in the wide variety of books and types of literature in the Bible to maintain a basic ethical norm from which decisions and actions should follow. As some have pointed out, the decision regarding diversity in ethical standards is as much a result from a prior methodological decision as is the search for unity and harmony of standards.

Recognizing the variety in the biblical message, we nevertheless believe we can find consistent unity regarding the message of God's revelation in Jesus Christ, the character of God, and His will for His people. This serves as the proper basis for answering the questions: "What is good?" "What ought we to do in order to do what is good, just, and right?"

Several basic assumptions are foundational for this conclusion. We believe the Bible's teaching has a unity about it so that it presents a consistent response to the questions raised in its various parts. Secondly, we affirm that the Bible, as God's inspired and authoritative Word, is intended to direct our actions and behavior. Finally, we can apply the moral statements in Scripture across cultures to all people, at all times, in all conditions.

This means every biblical teaching, whether it appears in a law code, narrative text, a prophetic section, a Gospel, or an epistle, originally was addressed to someone in a particular situation. Such particulars do not necessarily limit the Bible's usage in other times by other people, however. We believe that underlying each specific injunction is a universal principle. Thus, when we discover the general principle, the Scripture offers us direction for our day on specific decisions or issues such as the environmental crisis.

That which gives unity, harmony, and consistency to the ethical teachings of the Bible is the character and will of God. What God desires for His people grows out of who He is, what He has spoken, and what He has done. That being the case, how can we develop an ethic concerning the environment?

Doctrine and Ethics

We have observed that the ethical contents of the Bible are not offered in isolation from the doctrinal teaching of the Bible. The biblical doctrines that speak to the issue of the environment are creation, dominion, the Fall, and redemption. Let us turn our attention to these four important themes.

Creation

Some Christians have hesitated to become involved with environmental concerns for fear that these matters are wrapped up with "New Age" thought or "process theology." It is true that those committed to "the green movement" or "New Age" ideas have done much good in behalf of the environment. The positive element in this statement is the recognition that people are beginning to see that environmental issues are not merely technical but are basically spiritual. Evangelical Christians often have failed to respond to these vital issues because we have faulty understanding of the biblical doctrine. In our infatuation with scientific theories and the age of the earth, we have lost sight of the theological significance of this foundational biblical teaching.

The whole bedrock of environmental care is that God is the Creator of heaven and earth. The entire creation is an expression of God. As we grow in our understanding of creation, we learn about our Creator. This is why Paul declares that we can understand God's eternal attributes from what He has made (Rom. 1:20). We are not, however, to identify God with His creation. God is distinct from, and yet vitally involved in, His creation.

This affirmation separates a Christian view of creation from a process view or a New Age type of pantheism. In the other approaches God is *not* distinguished from His creation. Pantheism affirms that all matter/events are in God; He is not external to them.

Likewise, pantheism denies that creation is *ex nihilo.* Creation, for the New Age thinker or the process theologian, is both *ex materia* (out of matter) and out of God. This then leaves them with the conclusion that matter or event is eternal and preexistent. It has become as God. The picture has become the artist.[1]

Having affirmed that creation is distinct from God and that creation is out of nothing, we also must recognize it as good. The earth is God's good creation. These affirmations answer the question of why we should care about environmental issues. We do not attempt to inform ourselves and prompt one another to action simply because the earth is necessary for human and global survival. While this is true in itself, the church and Christian theology offer a more foundational and wide-reaching affirmation. We should care for the earth because it reflects the goodness of God Himself. The Bible maintains everything God created is "good" (Gen. 1:4, 10, 12, 18, 21, 25). The creation account concludes that it is in fact "very good" (Gen. 1:31).

A Christian view of creation not only recognizes that God is before all things, it gladly affirms that God created *all* things. Not only the Genesis account, but also the New Testament maintains God created *all* things (Eph. 3:9; Col. 1:16, 17; cf. Rom. 11:36). God the Father, God the Son, and God the Holy Spirit (the Triune Godhead) brought the created world into existence. God the Father is the source, planner, and originator of this world (Gen. 1:1; 1 Cor. 8:6). God the Son is the agent, the One doing the action or work of creation (John 1:3; Col. 1:16; Heb. 1:2). God the Spirit is the One lovingly hovering over the earth giving it shape and beauty (cf. Gen. 1:2).

A Christian view of creation acknowledges the world was created by the power of His Word (Ps. 33:6; 148:5) in accordance with His wisdom (Jer. 10:12) and His will (Rev. 4:11). God has revealed Himself in His good creation (Ps. 19:1; Rom. 1:20), and the creation brings glory to God (Isa. 43:7; Rev. 4:11).

A recognition of these important truths enables us to understand that the earth's beauty and value are not happenstance. The Creator purposefully built them into the creation. Thus, any attack on this inherent goodness is more than an attack against the earth. It is an attack against the Creator and thus is a form of blasphemy. The biblical approach to the environmental issue unapologetically affirms the earth is the Lord's (Ps. 24:1). God is the earth's Creator and, by right of creation, its owner. But the Bible adds another aspect to this foundational truth. Psalm 115:16 tells us God has given the earth to men and women. This brings us to our second theme: God has put humankind on earth to care for it, to work it, and to have dominion over it (Gen. 1:28; 2:15).

Dominion

On the sixth day of creation God created the living creatures. The culmination of this activity was creation of humanity and its subsequent mandate to rule over the animals and to subdue the earth. This concept of dominion has opened up Christianity to accusations of being anthropocentric, and thus being able to dispense with and dispose of nature as it sees fit.

The most influential proponent of this view is the much-quoted Lynn White, Jr.[2] White argued that the Judeo-Christian view of dominion paved the way for the science and technology that created the environmental crisis. He maintained : (1) the Bible establishes a dualism of humanity and nature; (2) the Bible is anthropocentric (literally, not just in the generic sense), thus no item in physical creation has any purpose except to serve humanity's purpose; and (3) it is God's will that humanity exploit (have dominion over) nature for its own ends.[3]

Why has the biblical concept of dominion been so misunderstood? Dominion is based on Genesis 1:28 and the meaning of two Hebrew words: *kabas* ("subdue") and *radah* ("rule over"). *Kabas* is a very strong term, which, in certain contexts such as Esther 7:8, can be translated "rape" or "molest." *Radah* is equally strong and can be understood as "trample."[4] Despite the strength of these words, they do not provide humanity with a mandate to dominate or conquer nature. These words must be interpreted, not according to their derivations, but according to their context.

The context makes one thing immediately obvious. Creation does not merely exist for humanity; it ultimately is for God's glory. All things exist for and have their meaning in God.

The creation story presents a balanced picture. Creation belongs to God because He made it. Creation belongs to humanity because God gave it to us. God has not handed the earth over to us in such a final way that He does not continue to maintain rights and control over it. He gave it to us to rule in His behalf.

Yet, our rulership is not without limits. The call for humanity to carry out the cultural mandate (Gen. 1:26-28) involves developing and unfolding the creation as the image-bearer of God.[5] Constraints regarding dominion immediately follow in the context (Gen. 1:29-30). Throughout the Pentateuch we find additional limitations:

- Fields are not to be reaped to the border (Lev. 19:9).
- The grower may only harvest from trees five years old (Lev. 19:25).
- The land is to lie idle regularly (Lev. 25:1-12).
- All the tithe of the land is the Lord's (Lev. 27:30-33).
- Fruit trees may not be used for siege works (Deut. 20:19).
- A mother bird is not to be taken with her young (Deut. 22:6).
- An ox is not to be muzzled when treading corn (Deut. 25:4).

Contrary to White's charges, it is evident that the Bible does not teach that God wills for humans to exploit nature for their own ends.

The ethical significance of dominion means God has placed men and women here to take care of God's good creation. We do not create its fertility; we encourage it. We are to protect it and keep it in good order. Our possession of the earth is a leasehold. We are only tenants. God continues to serve as the Lord of the land, the literal landlord. Just as creation's ultimate end is to bring glory to God, so our ultimate purpose is to glorify God in our care and dominion of the earth.

The dominion we humans have over the earth is derived from our unique relationship with God. God has placed men and women, who are created in His image, between Himself as Creator and the rest of creation. We are a part of creation, for we have been created. Yet, we are distinct and different because, unlike the rest of creation, we have been created in God's image. We breathe and reproduce like animals. We, however, pray, think, reason, love, and exercise dominion, which places our experience on a different level than that of animals. In this relationship we combine the capacities of dependence on God and dominion over and care for the earth.

The psalmist indicates humans are crowned with glory and honor in a unique way (Ps. 8). Of course, God's glory is of a different kind and degree altogether; His is far grander. But the psalmist, in harmony with the Genesis account, affirms a cooperative dominion. God deserves praise and glory because He cares about His creatures, including men and women, but God has crowned humans with glory as His vice-regents (Ps. 8:5-7).

Humans, therefore, are to manage the earth. They can and should continue to look for new ways to improve and accelerate the care of the earth. This, however, at best is an artificial management of essentially natural processes. It is only in cooperation with God that we cultivate the earth. Scripture suggests that God has humbled Himself in order to "cooperate" in this cultivation. But more importantly, we must humble ourselves by confessing that our dominion over nature is entirely fruitless if God ceased making the earth fruitful, thus continuing to give the earth increase.

Theologically, we affirm God not only as Creator but also as providential preserver (Col. 1:17; 1 Tim. 6:13; Heb. 1:3). By "providential" we mean God's continuing work whereby He controls all things in the universe, thereby bringing about the fulfillment of His wise plan. To confess God as preserver is to acknowledge His work of maintaining and protecting the existence of the created universe. This is accomplished by the very nature of His creative work and by His continuing loving care and gracious intervention.

If these things are true, as the Bible and the classic Christian confessions maintain, why does the present environmental crisis face us? What has gone wrong? The problem and lack of stability in our ecosystem can be traced back to a problem described in the initial chapters of Genesis. The problem with the environment is that the good creation now is imperfect (Gen. 3).

The Fall

While the doctrine of creation sets out theocentric ideals, it is the doctrine of the Fall that provides the most powerful analysis of life as we know it today. Adam and Eve's disobedience had immediate and long-term effects: "Cursed is the ground because of you . . ." (Gen. 3:17, NIV). But the problem is not just in the environment, it is primarily in all of us (Isa. 53:6).

Our task of living in the image of God as stewards, however, has become deformed. In human attempts to become autonomous, the man's and woman's sin resulted in the perversion of the whole order of nature in heaven and earth. The whole of creation was disrupted. The peace that existed in the garden between God, humanity, and nature was greatly disturbed. In the Fall lie the roots of our ecological crisis.

The task of fulfilling the cultural mandate becomes extremely complex. Being directed to become fruitful and fill the earth becomes a painful task (Gen. 3:16). Subduing the earth becomes painful and taxing (Gen. 3:17). Rulership becomes misunderstood and misdirected (Gen. 3:16). The creatureliness of humanity is underscored: *Adam* is *adamah* (cf. Gen. 4:10-14; Hos. 4:1-3).[6]

Throughout the Old Testament are examples of God's continual concern for all of His creation. The story of Noah is a case in point (Gen. 6-9).[7] God promised that a flood never again would destroy the earth. This clearly illustrates God's concern for the earth. This further is exemplified with the practices related to the sabbath year (Lev. 25:2-5) and the year of jubilee (Lev. 25:23).[8]

Since the time when humanity was banished from the garden and when Cain slew Abel, disarray and disorder have characterized the earth.

Redemption

Against this somber background, God's redeeming intervention provides an escape route from moral despair. Ethically, the Bible's doctrine of redemption comes to bear on the environmental issue in at least four points:

1. The doctrine of redemption which heals and changes fallen men and women so they can know God and follow His will.

2. Redemption, which provides enablement and motivation to do right and avoid wrong.

3. Establishment of goals for moral living.

4. Direction to a source of supernatural power which strengthens the failing human will.

The cross of Christ lies at the heart of redemption. The cross also is central to a Christian environmental ethic. This particularly is apparent in Colossians 1:15-20 and Romans 8:18-25.

Paul's message in Colossians 1 that *all things* have been reconciled to God by the cross of Christ cannot be restricted only to human beings. Nothing, except the continually disobedient who follow the path of Satan, is exempt from the reconciling power of the cross. The potential of reconciliation exists for all aspects of creation.[9]

The work of Jesus on the cross undermines any spirit/matter or nature/grace dualism. It declares that the creation itself also is worth dying for. Humanity is to be redeemed with creation, not apart from it. Paul claims in Romans 8 that creation has been subjected to futility, through humanity's sin, and will be liberated. The children of God will be given the privilege of releasing the fallen creation into the liberty that they themselves experience because of Jesus' work on the cross.[10]

The redemption of the earth will be accomplished when God brings about the new heaven and the new earth (Rev. 21). But during this interim period our responsibility as the redeemed people is to exercise redemptive dominion. If we think of the earth as a kingdom, then we are not kings ruling the territory, but we are vice-regents caring for and redeeming the territory in the King's behalf. We must share the fruit of the land with our needy neighbors. This in no way implies any type of Marxism, but it affirms the right of private property. Yet, we must see the right to private property as the right to common use and common good.

Our work as redeemed people places us in responsible positions of stewardship. We are not to understand dominion as destruction of the earth. On the contrary, it is a redemptive, responsible and productive management of the earth for future generations. We must celebrate our creativity and look for avenues to carry out the work of the redemption and preservation of the earth.

Ethics and Exposition

What are the implications of these four doctrinal and ethical themes for the church? How do the implications of these matters affect how we respond to the issues currently facing us in our world? In this last section I want to help us see how to establish a four-part sermon series for our churches based on the previous section. Certainly sermons are more than information; they also include exhortation, application, and illustration.[11] The following sermon outlines will only help us get started.

Sermon One:

God's Good Creation (Gen. 1:1-31)

Thesis: We recognize that everything has worth and value because it is a part of God's good creation. He created this world and was pleased to do so. Creation was good in His sight. God loves His creation, and we must have a concern for it, not just parts of it. We must avoid two traps: (1) We must not think the earth and related issues are unimportant because the earth is not divine. (2) We must not worship the earth but must worship the Creator of the earth. We should address all praise and honor to Him.

I. What is a Christian view of creation?

a. Creation is out of nothing

b. Creation is distinct from God

II. How is it different from false views of creation?

a. New Age ideas

b. Process theology

III. What are the practical implications of recognizing the value and beauty of God's earth?

Sermon Two:

Dominion: Dominance or Stewardship of the Environment (Gen. 1:26-28)

Thesis: We must accept our responsibility as stewards. We are to preserve, guard, and develop what God has created. God designed that men and women should govern the earth for its good and have dominion over it to care for it and to use it for human needs. Everything God has made has its function in God's wise providential plan. Our role is to care for the rest of creation. Rather than being at the back of the line in dealing with ecological concerns, God's people should be at the very front. Our concerns grow out of our recognition that the earth is the Lord's and that He has given us its stewardship.

I. What do we mean by dominion?

II. What are the limitations of dominion?

III. What is the relationship between dependence on God and dominion over the earth?

IV. How do we carry out our roles as managers and stewards of the earth?

Sermon Three:

The Environmental Problem (Gen. 3)

Thesis: The task of stewardship has been deformed. In our attempt to become autonomous we have disobeyed God and defaced His creation. The whole order of creation has been perverted. The problem with the environment ultimately is a problem with humankind. The roots of our ecological crisis lie in a much deeper place than the "New Age" or "green movement" suggests. The problem is with us, our sin, and our rebellion toward God.

I. Why have we failed in our stewardship of the earth?

II. How has our sin affected the environment?

III. How can we know God still is concerned with His world?

IV. What are the implications of our disobedience toward God for addressing the environmental crisis?

Sermon Four:

Our Renewed Responsibility for the Environment (Rom. 8:18-25)

Thesis: If we recognize the need for redemption, then we understand our need for repentance. The problems related to the environment are not just related to the soul, to technology, or to science, but to us. We must confess that we have not cared for God's creation as we should. We have abused our responsibilities of dominion and stewardship. We have mistreated the land and its people, our neighbors, friends, and family. We humbly repent of our wrong, turn from our failures, and live out our discipleship more responsibly.

I. How does the cross of Christ impact our responsibility for the environment?

II. What part should repentance play in the construction of a Christian environmental ethic?

III. How does the promise of a new heaven and new earth inform our present responsibilities as redeemed stewards?

Conclusion

We praise our God who has created us and redeemed us. We acknowledge that the only true deliverance for ourselves and our earth is in Christ, our Creator and Savior. We are not faced with paradoxical choices: to follow Christ or be caretakers of the earth. To follow Christ completely involves responding as the Holy Spirit leads us in our communities to deal with the earth's environmental problems. Those who blame the environmental problems on basic beliefs of the Christian faith do not understand the biblical teachings regarding creation, dominion, and redemption.

It is good that the church has become concerned in recent years about the future of the earth. But we have only begun. These are positive steps, but it is important for us to continue. We must affirm and proclaim a full-orbed gospel that includes the creation mandate and the teachings of the New Testament. We must put these principles into practice in creative ways, but we always must maintain these biblical, theological, and ethical underpinnings. Then we one day will know that the biblical message of redemption from sins also promises redemption for God's good earth.[12]

Notes

1. Steve Bishop, "Green Theology and Deep Ecology: New Age or New Creation?" *Themelios* 16 (April/May, 1991), 8.

2. Lynn White, Jr., "The Historical Roots of Ecological Crisis," *Science* 155 (March 10, 1967), 1203-07. More recently White's thesis has been amplified by Andree Collard, *Rape of the Wild* (1989), and Ian L. McHarg, *Design with Nature* (1989).

3. White's work has been challenged and refuted several times. See Robin Attfield, *The Ethics of Environmental Concern* (London: Blackwell, 1983); Stephen V. Monsma, ed. *Responsible Technology* (Grand Rapids: Eerdmans, 1986).

4. See Gerhard Von Rad, *Genesis* (London: SCM, 1972), 60-61; Claus Westermann, *Genesis 1-11* (London: SPCK, 1974), 142-57.

5. Douglas J. Hall, *Imaging God* (Grand Rapids: Eerdmans, 1986), 61-112.

6. Michael Deroche, "The Reversal of Creation in Hosea," *Vetus Testamentum* 31 (1981), 403.

7. Noah perhaps was the first conservationist. See Richard Bauckham, *The Bible and Politics* (London: SPCK, 1989), 16.

8. See Robert B. Sloan, *The Favorable Year of the Lord* (Missoula, MT: Scholars, 1977); M.H. Woudstra, "The Year of Jubilee and Related Old Testament Laws—Can They Be 'Translated' for Today?" *Theological Forum* 5 (1977), 1-21.

9. See Richard R. Melick, Jr., *Philippians, Colossians, Philemon* (NAC; Nashville: Broadman, 1991), 228-29.

10. See Douglas Moo, *Romans 1-8* (Wycliffe; Chicago: Moody, 1991), 547-59.

11. See my section on "From Text to Sermon" in *Hermeneutics and Preaching*, ed. Raymond Bailey (Nashville: Broadman, 1992).

12. Portions of this chapter were taken from my article, "Creation, Dominion, Redemption: A Christian View of the Environment," *Search* (1992) and used with permission.

8

A Denominational Perspective on Biblical Stewardship

William M. Pinson, Jr.

The subject of this chapter naturally falls into three parts: biblical stewardship, God's resources, and a denominational perspective. Each is related to the other. Let us examine each individually and then see how together they bear on our responsibility as witnesses of the Lord Jesus Christ in a terribly corrupt and lost world.

Biblical Stewardship

Biblical stewardship begins where anything biblical begins, and that is with God. The central idea in the Bible concerning stewardship is that God is the Creator and Owner of all that is. As Genesis declares, "In the beginning God created the heaven and the earth" (Gen. 1:1, KJV). We human beings—part of all that God created—relate as stewards or trustees to that which God has brought into being. J. E. Dillard reminded us that "Bible stewardship is the acknowledgment of God's ownership, the acceptance of our trusteeship of life and possessions, and the administration of the same according to the will of God."[1]

Bobby Eklund, in his booklet "Biblical Doctrine of Stewardship," indicates three words capsule the biblical teaching on stewardship: trustee, steward, and partner. Each of these relates not only to the concept of God as Creator but also as Sustainer, Judge, and Redeemer. God has created all that is and sustains what He has created; in Him we live and move and have our being, as Paul said to the Athenians. He has placed in our trust what He has created and sustains. The Christian as trustee is one to whom something special has been entrusted with the confidence that it

126

will be kept and protected. The Christian also is to be a steward. As such, the believer is an administrator, or a manager, of what God has placed in his or her possession. We are not merely to keep safely what God has entrusted to us, but we also are to actively manage it according to God's will and purpose. As James Leo Garrett has pointed out, "God's ownership of all things and man's relative but real dominion over lower creatures lead in biblical thought to man's obligation to a responsible management or use of material things."[2] And God as Judge holds us accountable for our trusteeship and stewardship.

God also is Redeemer. Too often the discussion of biblical stewardship centers almost exclusively on God as Creator, ignoring or giving short shrift to the biblical emphasis on God as Redeemer. William Hendricks reminds us, "No evangelical Christian would overlook the necessity of beginning every discussion about God at the point where his Word initiated conversation with us, namely in redemption."[3] Hendricks further states that an appropriate starting point for a discussion of Christian stewardship is creation as seen from the viewpoint of redemption. "This means that we are first those who have been grasped by God and, in reflecting on the meaning of this, we observe that the God who grasps men in Jesus Christ has fashioned man and the world. Expressed theologically, this is to say that the redeemer God is the creator God."[4]

God, having provided redemption for us through the gift of His Son, calls us into partnership with Him to take the Good News about that redemption to all persons everywhere. He has entrusted to us not only the gospel but also the ministry of reconciliation. Hendricks writes:

The New Testament concept of stewardship is based on God's redemptive plan itself. It involves the body of Christ as composed of Christians who become a living temple in which God dwells through his Spirit (Eph. 2:20-22). The upbuilding or edification of fellow believers is as intrinsic a part of stewardship as is being a steward of the mysteries of the gospel. This means Christian stewardship is involved with evangelism and Christian growth. Only when this wider basis for stewardship is recognized may one speak about the stewardship of substance. The biblical premise is that life and all of its substance and experiences belong to God because He has made, sustained, and permitted them.[5]

James Leo Garrett states well the missionary purpose of stewardship:

The stewardship of material things for Christians includes more than the right use and conservation of natural resources and the limitation of environmental pollution. Material things, when freely and gratefully dedicated and given to God and entrusted to the Christian"household of faith," can and should be so utilized by Christian persons in the service of Christ and the fellowship of his church as to be means and instruments employed and empowered by the Holy Spirit for Christian evangelization, Christian instruction and nurture, and Christian helping ministries. Such gifts sustain both the enablers who seek to equip all Christians for their ministries and the emissaries of the good news of Christ who plant the need for new fellowships of the reborn.

With no Gnostic or Manichaean disdain, no Hindu or Buddhist detachment, and no Marxist or capitalist obsession, Christians as stewards of material things—as well as of the gospel and of their total lives—can participate responsibly and joyfully in the transformation of material things into spiritual reality through Jesus Christ, His gospel, His Spirit, and His church.[6]

God has provided us with all of the resources we need to carry out our partnership responsibility. We are to be good stewards of the resources entrusted to us. Thus, "a steward is one who has received a trust from God and is in partnership with God through Christ for the working out of God's purposes for humankind."[7]

And what are the resources God entrusted to us to carry out His redemptive purposes? In short, all that is—both the material and the spiritual. Biblical stewardship must take into account all of these, for the Bible presents all of them as entrusted to our care. They all are from God and belong to God. We are stewards, not owners, of these. The resources God has entrusted to us include:

natural resources;
plant and animal life;
human life;
what humans produce, utilizing natural resources, plants, and animals;
abilities bestowed upon us by God; and
God's special spiritual resources.

Let us examine briefly each of these precious resources which God has provided.

God's Resources

All of the resources that went into making our possessions came from God, and all belong to God. Although we never should forget that we are but stewards, we often do. We often relate to the created order in an anthropocentric rather than a theocentric fashion. Such self-centeredness and disobedience are sinful. The wages of sin always is death. The cause-and-effect relation of sin and death under God's judgment seldom is more vividly illustrated than in our relationship to the world God has made.

Consider, for example, what we term natural resources—the atmosphere, earth, water, and other inanimate pieces of creation such as minerals. All of this is necessary for life—human and other—and composes a resource for us to use according to God's direction and for His glory. We are to manage it so that future generations benefit from it. We are to be partners with God in using it to produce that which enhances life.

Misusing these natural resources is sin and brings forth God's judgment. For example, when Jeremiah isolated one of Israel's acts of disobedience, which was bringing about the Babylonian exile, he selected as an example the exploitation of their land (Jer. 25:11,12; 29:10). God had commanded Israel to work the land in cycles of six years, allowing it to rest during the seventh year (Lev. 25:1-7; Ex. 23:10-11). The purpose of this likely was twofold. One was practical, to allow the land to rebuild itself. The other was theological, to remind the people that the land belonged to God and that they were stewards of it. But Israel did not obey God. Bible scholar Ray Summers points out that as a result, Jeremiah said, "God would see to it that the land got its Sabbath—even if it had to get it all at once! Babylon would carry Israel away captive. This would last seventy years. In a rather general way of reckoning, that would be one-seventh of the time Israel had disobeyed God in exploiting the very land which He had put under its stewardship. The land would have its Sabbath."[8]

A similar exploitation of natural resources has brought many woes on our world today. We should heed the word of the Lord: "The wilderness and the dry land shall be glad, the desert shall rejoice and blossom; like the crocus it shall blossom abundantly, and rejoice with joy and singing" (Isa. 35:2, RSV)—when the earth is treated with good stewardship.

Similarly, the Bible views animal and plant life as belonging to God and given to humankind to use as a resource in God's service and for His glory. The Genesis account of creation makes this clear, as do numerous other passages. The psalmist sums it up this way: "The earth is the Lord's, and the fullness thereof; the world, and they that dwell therein" (Ps. 24:1, KJV). God in his Word expresses concern for animal life: "Thou shall not muzzle the ox when he treadeth out the corn" (Deut. 25:4, KJV); and for plant life: "When thou shalt besiege a city a long time, in making war against it to take it, thou shalt not destroy the trees thereof by forcing an ax against them" (Deut. 20:19, KJV).

Often right-to-life advocates emphasize human life alone, but we need to remember that human life cannot exist in isolation from other forms of life. We depend on those other forms of life. Our concern for the vast array of life forms should stem not only from the fact that they are part of God's creation but also because the existence of human life, the crown of creation, depends on these other life forms. Russell E. Train, Chairman of the World Wildlife Fund and the Conservation Foundation, speaks vividly of this interrelation of natural resources, animal and plant life, and human life:

We depend upon the air to supply us with the oxygen we must breathe—oxygen that in turn is produced by the microrganisms in the surface of the ocean and by the vegetative cover of the land, particularly its tropical forests, often referred to as the lungs of the plant. We depend for our sustenance on the productivity of the soil, whose fertility is in turn sustained by the nitrogen-fixing ability of soil bacteria. The humus essential to productive soils is of course the product of the work of other bacteria, beetles, worms, and such. (Size is clearly no measure of the importance of one's role in the planetary scheme. In fact, it is truly the little things that run the world!) Our grains and other crops, our orchards and much of the world's forests depend for pollination and, thus, their continued existence upon insects, birds and bats among other mammals—often highly specialized to serve the needs of a particular species of plant.[9]

Unfortunately, our stewardship record in relation to plant and animal life is poor indeed.

Human life in all of its variety and essential parts—physical, spiritual, mental, emotional, and social—is another resource God has provided for us and another for which we are responsible as stewards—our life and the lives of others. Human life is especially precious because human beings are created in the image of God. This places heavy responsibility on us for the care and treatment of the life God has given us and others. All aspects of human life must be important because Scripture records that Jesus grew in wisdom, and stature, and in favor with God and with other human beings. He also taught that the body is the temple of the Holy Spirit (1 Cor. 6:19-20). Perhaps this total stewardship responsibility for human life is behind Jesus' declaration in response to the question of what was the greatest commandment: "Thou shalt love the Lord thy God with all thy heart, and with all thy soul, and with all thy mind. This is the first and great commandment. And the second is like unto it, Thou shalt love thy neighbor as thyself" (Matt. 22:37-39, KJV).

Our record of responsible stewardship of the resource of human life is no better and perhaps no worse than that in relation to other resources. Consider the stewardship of the individual human life. Concerning the physical, many overeat and underexercise, ingest destructive substances, and expose themselves to physical harm. Concerning the spiritual, many ignore the call to salvation and plunge on in sinful rebellion to eternal damnation, while others who claim to have experienced God's saving grace live little better than the avowed unbeliever, stunting their spiritual growth with lack of any kind of spiritual discipline. Concerning the mind, most fill it with inanity at best or with soul-polluting input at worst; few use the marvelous resource of the human mind to capacity, proving to be poor stewards indeed. Unfortunately, our emotional selves are treated no better.

Our generally poor pattern of stewardship for our own lives is matched, if not exceeded, by that of our relation to other persons and to the organizations and institutions of society. What marvelous resources God has provided in interpersonal relationships, in family life, in the structures of our economic and political life, and in organizations intended for recreation. What reprehensible stewards many of us are in regard to these, and what a terrible price we pay for our sin. Injustice, racial prejudice and discrimination, inadequate housing, education, medical care, divorce and delinquency, pornography and prostitution, greed and thievery all take a terrible toll on what God intended to be resources for our good and His glory.

What is produced by human effort relating to the resources God has put at our disposal—intelligence and energy in individuals, structures and organizations in society, animal and plant life, and natural resources—is another resource for which God holds us responsible—the fruit of our labor including money and other forms of wealth, houses and public buildings, art and literature. God warned Israel—and through them us—that such belonged to God also and was to be regarded as God's, not ours:

> When thou hast eaten and art full, then thou shalt bless the Lord
> thy God for the good land which he hath given thee. Beware that
> thou forget not the Lord thy God, in not keeping his command-
> ments, and his judgments, and his statutes, which I command thee
> this day: Lest when thou hast eaten and art full, and hast built
> goodly houses, and dwelt therein, and when thy herds and thy
> flocks multiply, and thy silver and thy gold is multiplied, and all
> that thou hast is multiplied; then thine heart be lifted up, and thou
> forget the Lord thy God . . . and thou say in thine heart, my power
> and the might of mine hand hath gotten me this wealth. But thou
> shalt remember the Lord thy God: for it is he that giveth thee
> power to get wealth, that he may establish his covenant which he
> sware unto thy fathers, as it is this day (Deut. 8:10-18, KJV).

Clearly, many are poor stewards of the things that human effort
produces by utilizing the resources of God. Greed, misplaced priorities, and selfish opulence in the midst of vast human need each
highlight our disobedience to God's command.

Besides these resources from God which primarily are part of
the material order of existence, God has provided us resources
which may be termed more spiritual, such as the Bible, the Holy
Spirit, the church, and spiritual gifts for ministry, service, and
stewardship. Of course, these are by no means isolated from the
other resources regarded as material. In fact, these spiritual resources enable us to be faithful stewards of the material resources.

For example, the Holy Spirit is given to us to empower us in
witness and ministry, to comfort us as we serve God in a hostile
world, and to guide and teach us as we use other resources at our
disposal, such as the church, the Bible and spiritual gifts. Furthermore certain spiritual gifts seem to relate very directly to our stewardship responsibilities for the created order in which we live. For
example, the Bible indicates that God gave to humankind dominion (Gen. 2). The psalmist declares of humankind, "Thou madest
him to have dominion over the works of thy hands; thou hast put
all things under his feet" (Ps. 8:6, KJV).

Dominion did not mean God gave human beings the right to

plunder and rape the earth but rather gave them the responsibility to dress and to keep it. Stewardship places the powers of dominion in service to the creation. Before the Fall we had a single job, to keep the garden. "Earth stewardship is therefore the primal human task."[10] In order that dominion could be rightfully exercised, God gifted humankind with wisdom and rulership.

Properly used, these spiritual resources can enable us to relate in loving governance to all creatures. However, sin has crippled our capacity for proper dominion and has afflicted the natural order as well. We live in a fallen state and can never return the earth to perfection. That must await the working of God's grace through the redemption provided by His Son, our Saviour, the Lord Jesus Christ (Rom. 8:19-23) in the coming of a new heaven and a new earth prophesied by Isaiah (Isa. 65:17) and witnessed by John (Rev. 21:1). In the meantime, we are to use our spiritual gifts to be as good stewards as possible, acknowledging our sin and claiming the promises of God's grace.

A Denominational Perspective and Response

Part of the way we exercise our stewardship responsibilities is through structure and organization, including that of our denomination. Surely Christians as individuals and through churches and denominations should be busy endeavoring not only to be good stewards of the resources God has given us but also to be busy correcting the ecological disasters resulting from poor stewardship. However, the observation of many who are deeply involved in ecological issues is that religious groups have been little involved. Russell Train, in a speech delivered before the North American Conference on Religion and Ecology in 1990 in Washington, commented, "Here we have problems that can be said to threaten the very integrity of creation. And yet the churches and other institutions of organized religion have largely ignored the whole subject."[11]

An article in *Christianity Today* in 1989 stated that at a recent forum on "Contributions of the New Testament to Christian Environmental Stewardship," University of Wisconsin graduate student David Wise said that in his extensive survey of literature on this topic he found only six significant New Testament-based writings on the environment, only one of which was written after 1972.[12] However, leaders in the Christian ecological movement report that in the past two or three years Christians "have become aware that this issue is one of direct importance to them and have also begun asking how they should respond."[13]

Indeed, how should we as a denomination respond? Since biblical stewardship is total stewardship—the responsible care of all that we are and possess as a trust from God to be used according to His plan and purpose—a denominational response should be total. This means that we should apply the biblical principles of stewardship to all of God's resources.

It also means that all aspects of our denomination should be brought to bear on the problems and opportunities, including individuals; churches; associations of churches; encampments; state convention entities such as schools, children's homes, hospitals and institutions for the aging; and national entities such as boards, commissions, seminaries, and other agencies. The Christian Life Commission could draft a master plan involving all of these entities, relating them to the biblical stewardship of all the resources God has provided.

A denominational response certainly should set forth both a theological and ethical basis for concern and action as well as a practical plan for specific response by each denominational entity to all of the problems and challenges related to each resource—the atmosphere, soil, water, minerals, plants, animals, human life, the results of production and spiritual resources.

A fully developed, systematic theological and ethical basis for a biblical stewardship of all God's resources apparently is lacking in our denomination. We need such a statement. It should be thoroughly biblical; that is the way Baptists—or anyone for that matter—should approach theology and ethics. And no excuse exists for it not to be biblical. As Stephen Muratore points out, the Bible is the

> operating manual for spaceship earth provided by the manufac-
> turer. This is authoritative! Let us look into the original operating
> manual for spaceship earth for the precepts of earth stewardship.
> The Bible is surprisingly rich in them. Perhaps we have to see it
> with new eyes, or listen to it with fresher ears, and clear our minds
> of the encrustations of churchianity, but let us have no doubt that
> there is ecological wisdom herein.[14]

The Bible primarily is our guide to basics, not specific action for the twentieth century. As Loren Wilkinson points out, "The Bible is not a textbook. It does not tell us how we in the twentieth centu-ry are to conduct our land use, energy and trade policies. It does, however, give us certain principles, relevant to all times, which we must seek to understand and apply to our own situations."[15]

Certainly a theology of ecology will explore how all the primary doctrines of the Christian faith relate to this issue. God as Creator, Sustainer, Judge, and Redeemer is a proper beginning place. Cor-rectly understood, the biblical doctrine of God will lead away from heretical extremes such as pantheism, which leads to a wor-ship of the created world rather than the Creator, or deism, which separates God from His creation so far that believing it we could never sing, "This is my Father's world. . . ." The biblical viewpoint is that God is the creator and owner of all that is and has entrusted a part of His creation to us for responsible management; He holds us accountable, and we must expect to give an account of our stew-ardship of all the resources He has placed at our disposal.

Similarly, the biblical doctrine of Christ will help us understand the true nature of our stewardship, for the Bible presents Jesus as the Agent, Lord and Redeemer of creation. A careful study of oth-er biblical doctrines, such as humanity, sin, salvation, church and Holy Spirit, will reveal basic truths essential to an understanding of a biblical stewardship of God's resources. This understanding will provide the appropriate motivation for action. As Loren Wilkinson says in *Earth Keeping*, "The overriding motivation for such action rests, for Christians at least, in responsible stewardship—the task of caring for God's creation. We must act out of obedience to that task, not out of self-interest or even out of altruism."[16]

A second responsibility of the denomination is to become aware of the issues, problems, and challenges biblical stewardship confronts us with in light of the facts related to the abuse of the created order. Damage to the environment is not disputable; it is a fact. The nature and extent of that damage and the appropriate response of the follower of Jesus Christ in light of the Bible's teachings is information the denomination has an obligation to distribute not only to Baptists but to the population in general. And of course the information must be as accurate as possible both in terms of the Bible's teachings and the state of the resources God has given us, such as the environment.

The denomination can do much to develop this awareness. Scholars, researchers, professors, teachers, and writers can do the necessary research to provide the material required to inform us all. The information these persons gather can be disseminated by a multitude of persons in a variety of ways. Central to this spread of knowledge are the various agencies of the denomination which prepare material for reading and viewing and which conduct conferences and meetings of various kinds throughout the nation, such as the Sunday School and Home Mission Board, the various commissions, the seminaries, and the state conventions, including universities. Each of these needs to develop an intentionality related to preparing materials and planning conferences which deal with the principles and practice of biblical stewardship of all God's resources.

The Christian Life Commission through the years has been a leader in this effort. Writers and speakers for all Baptist entities should be encouraged to use information on total biblical stewardship. Without a steady stream of information on ecology and other stewardship concerns, the other aspects of a denominational strategy will be severely handicapped. These other aspects include programs of work and ministry by national and state conventions, associations, and local churches.

The annual meetings of state and national conventions and of associations afford opportunities for building awareness. People can do this through sermons and addresses, media presentations, displays in exhibit areas, and resolutions presented for consideration and adoption. For example, the Southern Baptist Convention has passed several such resolutions dealing with issues such as pollution of the environment, population, energy, and responsible use of natural resources. However, considering the magnitude of the issue, relatively little has been done at major conventions and meetings to heighten awareness.

Seminaries, universities, and other educational institutions certainly should be centers of influence for responsible total stewardship. Courses and seminars on the subject are a must. Special forums, lectureships, and conferences will help. A media center well stocked with related material can be a major asset.

Participation of churches is essential if the denomination is to have any widespread influence in developing an awareness of the issues related to stewardship and ecological concerns. Most churches frankly have done little, but they can do much. Preaching and teaching on the topic will reach the most people. Special conferences also can contribute. Available material in the church library, bulletin inserts, pamphlets in tract racks, and posters in the buildings all help build awareness.

The denomination can encourage individual and corporate action to deal with related problems. Through the various channels already mentioned should flow a steady stream of practical suggestions for individuals on how to be responsible stewards of God's resources. These can range from tips on recycling to measures for energy conservation in homes and travel to means of curtailing pollution. Some suggestions which may seem trivial actually are not; for example, as much energy leaks through American windows every year as flows through the Alaskan pipeline. The denomination also should encourage corporate action to deal with these matters.

Businesses and farmers, lawmakers and educators, corporations, and institutions ought to feel the influence of the denomination for responsible stewardship in their operations. One such means of bringing influence is through lobbying for adequate and reasonable laws helping to protect the environment. The moral issues on which we speak should include ecology as well as pornography and pollution as well as abortion. Another means is pressure on businesses to act responsibly toward the environment. Christians bring pressure on business to not sponsor programs on television which corrupt morals; why not bring pressure on businesses to not engage in practices corrupting the environment? Such pressure can have a positive effect, especially when the denomination displays a willingness to work with business in a partnership of responsible stewardship. Earle Harbison, the president of Monsanto, testified in an interview to the effect of environmentalists: "I take nothing away from the environmentalists. They brought pressure to bear on the entire environmental picture, and I take my hat off to some of the things they did."[17]

The denomination also should set an example for responsible stewardship. Each entity of the denomination ought to behave as a good steward. It may be that we are as guilty as any group of failing to practice biblical stewardship. Practicing what we preach about stewardship relates to individuals and to organizations. For example, individual Christians can set an example by how they care for their bodies, minds, emotions, and spiritual gifts; by how they practice conservation of energy in driving patterns and heating and cooling of their homes; by how they contribute to the environment by the products they use or refrain from using; and by participating in efforts to alter social circumstances that damage human life and potential.

Denominational organizations and institutions certainly ought to set an example of responsible biblical stewardship. This can be done in a variety of ways. Many of these can track the example of individuals. However, the practice of an organization or institution is in numerous ways even more important. The impact is greater, of course; energy conservation by a huge hospital or university makes more difference than that by an individual. Furthermore, the institution sets an example for a multitude of people, such as employees, users and observers. An agency, for example, that states it will reduce the number of conferences to which people must travel and will prioritize such events and utilize as much as possible alternate methods of sharing information in an effort to practice good stewardship will set an example for others to follow. By setting up a collection center for recycling to be used by employees, an institution sets an example that encourages employees and others to recycle. By rewarding good health practices by employees, an agency encourages stewardship of human life and sets an example for others. Clearly, the opportunities for denominational organizations to behave as good stewards of God's resources are numerous. And in doing this, they will encourage others to do likewise.

All our denomination does should help advance our Lord's Kingdom and bring glory to His name. Clearly, all efforts to put into effect biblical stewardship of all God's resources will do that. We must never forget that God is Redeemer as well as Creator. As Dan Vestal has written in *The Doctrine of Creation,*

> One who has come to know God through Jesus Christ and one who has by faith accepted Him as Creator as well as Redeemer will not view creation simply as a subject for philosophical discussion. Rather, such a one will view creation as a cause for celebration and worship.To think that the Creator God and Redeemer God are one and the same is, indeed, a reason to rejoice. To understand that creation is the platform for God's redemptive love is indeed a reason to rejoice. It is the Savior God who is worshiped. The Savior God is also the Creator God. Hallelujah![18]

Ecological concern and evangelistic zeal go together. We are to use the resources provided by the Creator God to share the gift of salvation of the Savior God. Our witness is damaged when we damage the world God has made and in which our fellow human beings must live. Love for God and others is expressed in love for God's creation and creatures. Our expressed concern for creation and our actions in its behalf help authenticate our presentation of the gospel. Much of our activity to care for creation aids missions and evangelism, enhancing the resources we have to carry the Good News to everyone everywhere. So let us be about our Father's business, caring for the creation He has placed in our trust, being good stewards of the mysteries of Christ, and participating in the partnership to which we have been called for the advancement of our Lord's Kingdom to His glory.

Notes

1. Henry A. Parker, "The Christian and the Economic Order," *Resource Unlimited*, ed. William L. Hendricks (Nashville: Stewardship Commission of the Southern Baptist Convention, 1972), 127.

2. James Leo Garrett, "A Christian View of Material Things," *Resource Unlimited*, 85.

3. William L. Hendricks, "The Context of Stewardship," *Resource Unlimited*, 5.

4. Ibid., 6.

5. William L. Hendricks, "The Christian and the Tithe," *Resource Unlimited*, 197.

6. Garrett, "A Christian View of Material Things," *Resource Unlimited*, 94.

7. Bobby L. Eklund, *Biblical Doctrine of Stewardship* (Dallas: Baptist General Convention of Texas, n.d.), 4.

8. Ray Summers, "Christian Stewardship in the Light of Redemption," in *Resource Unlimited*, 25 .

9. Russell E. Train, "Caring for Creation: Religion and Ecology," *Vital Speeches of the Day*, August 15, 1990, 665.

10. Stephen Muratore, "Earth Stewardship," *Epiphany* (Fall, 1989-Winter 1990), 127.

11. Train, "Caring for Creation," 664.

12. David Wise, "Ecology Theology," *Christianity Today*, September 22, 1989, 40.

13. "The Earth Moans, and Christians are Listening," *Christianity Today*, September 22, 1989, 38.

14. Muratore, "Earth Stewardship," 126.

15. Loren Wilkenson, *Earth Keeping* (Grand Rapids: Eerdmans, 1980), 251.

16. Ibid., 302.

17. Mark L. Schannon, "One Businessperson's View of the Ecological Crisis: The Restoration of Trust," *Vital Speeches of the Day*, January 1, 1991, 177.

18. Daniel Vestal, *The Doctrine of Creation* (Nashville: Convention, 1989), 14.

IV
The Homiletic Challenge

9

Accepting Our Responsibility

Jack N. Graham

Unfortunately, we in the evangelical church often are slow to accept our ethical and moral responsibilities. Nowhere is this more evident than on the issue of the environment. Evangelical literature on the subject is scarce. I must admit that in my own preaching I have done very little on the subject. Christian action in this area is minimal. Could it be that we have been so "heavenly minded that we are of no earthly good?"

We need to strike a balance between spiritual realities and secular earthly realities. As Christians, we live in two worlds. We live in the spiritual world of the Kingdom, and we live in a temporal world of here and now. While we are looking forward to the "land that is fairer than day," we also realize we have a responsibility to be concerned and to be connected with God's world today. While we live on tiptoe with expectancy for the land that is to be, we also must accept our serious and sobering responsibilities to take care of the world we now have.

Of all people, Christians should have compassion for the earth and for the environment. As believers we have a responsibility. The Bible specifically tells us that creation now groans and suffers. We must not seek to abdicate our responsibility to care for the beauty and the blessing of the earth. We must not walk by on the other side with the priest and the Levite while the earth is bleeding and hurting.

Some even accuse Christians of causing environmental abuse. People accuse us of abusing creation because of our arrogant and self-centered view of nature and the creation. Some people even suggest that we abandon Christian teaching as a foundation for ecology and environmental truth. People suggest New Age thought as the answer to our ecological questions.

If we as Christians do not get involved in this issue, the unbelieving world will think us uncaring and irrelevant. Many unbelievers already are wondering why we're not involved.

Our Responsibility to Future Generations

We say we care about the unborn, and I believe that we do. But what about the millions of unborn who face birth into a world facing environmental disaster? Are we responsible for securing not only the future generation's birth but also its life on earth? Obviously, we are. Do we have a right to speak? Do we have a responsibility to speak?

I believe we do because the Christian's world view is based upon biblical principles—God's revelation to humanity. And the Word of God has a message encompassing and including all of life. It includes life now, here, and in the hereafter. So we need to discover what God's Word says.

Francis Schaeffer has written: ". . . biblical Christianity has a real answer to the ecological crisis; it offers a balanced and healthy attitude to nature, arising from the truth of His creation by God. It offers the hope here and now of substantial healing in nature. . . ."[1]

We believe that God created the heavens and the earth. We believe He did that by *fiat*, "out of nothing," by the Word of His power. All things came to be by His Word. According to the New Testament, the incarnate Word, the living Word, and our Creator all are one—Christ Himself. Colossians 1:16-17, NIV says: "For by him all things were created: things in heaven and on earth, visible and invisible . . . all things were created by him [that is, Jesus] and for him. He is before all things, and in him all things hold together." Our Savior is the Christ of the cosmos. He is the God of the galaxy, and all of creation is for His purpose and for His pleasure and for His praise. He not only is the Christ of the cross but also the Christ of creation. He cares not only for the Christian, but

He cares for the creation. And the Scripture tells us that He even knows when a sparrow falls to the ground.

Our love for the Maker of the earth precedes our love for the earth. The reason we love this world is because it is God's world.

So the Christian's view of ecology and the environment is not one which is theoretical, not one which is philosophical, but one which is experiential. We claim to know the Creator personally. We believe in the One who made it all, and therefore we are twice blessed.

We know God by His general revelation that we see in the skies, the stars, the mountains, and the oceans. But we also know God and God's creation by special revelation and supernatural and strategic revelation—the Living Word, and the incarnate Word.

In Genesis 1:1 the creation account begins sublimely and simply. It introduces us to the Creator. The very first verse of the Bible says, "In the beginning God created the heavens and the earth." This challenges many ancient and modern foes—in particular that of paganism, polytheism, and pantheism. We discover in Genesis 1:1 that God is holy and is revealed as separate from the creation totally. This is important for us to understand because the greatest challenges of our times pertain to dualism and pantheism. Dualism is the notion that the universe resulted from two independent sources—one good and one evil. Dualistic thinking is present today in Eastern mysticism as well as in contemporary literature and even modern movies such as *Star Wars*. Pantheism is the idea that the universe and God essentially are the same; to speak of one is to speak of the other. Many environmentalists hold to this view of pantheism and thereby worship the creation rather than the Creator. This is idolatry; it is not the biblical Christian view.

The problem is that many times we have turned over the issue of the environment to the fanatical fringe while we remain silent in bringing to bear conservative biblical truth and revelation on this issue.

The Bible tells us that creation is for God's glory. His creation brings Him praise and honor. The earth, nevertheless, is the theater for the divine drama of redemption. "For God so loved the world, that He gave His only begotten Son" (John 3:16, KJV). Of course, God's primary focus is humanity, the world of people for whom Christ died. But we also must understand that the world for whom Christ died is the earth that suffers, the earth that is in pain, the earth that has been cursed as a result of humanity's sin. It, therefore, also needs redemption. Of all the planets and of all the peoples, God so loved the world. And the earth's origin and destiny are governed by God.

Materialism is not the answer to the problems of the environment. Secular and scientific humanism are not the solutions because the ultimate meaning and final destiny of humankind cannot be determined by the material but only by the eternal and the spiritual. The Bible begins with the statement of truth and fact: "In the beginning God created the heaven and the earth," and it ends with "new heavens and a new earth, wherein dwelleth righteousness" (2 Pet. 3:13, KJV). So the scriptural view, the biblical view, is that while God and His creation are totally separate, they are not isolated from one another.

God's Spirit, who created this world, continues to work in this world and sustain this world. The Word of His power upholds all things. The One who is the source of creation also is the sustainer of creation and the superintendent of creation. He did not speak and create the earth and then walk away, never to have anything to do with it again. He continually works in His creation. God's Spirit constantly is making and remaking through the process of nature.

Paul said in Acts 17:25, NIV: "And he is not served by human hands, as if he needed anything, because he himself gives all men life and breath and everything else." In other words, the God who created the earth cares about the earth. He controls the earth. His sustaining Spirit watches over it in constant compassion. If for one moment God's Spirit were to remove His hand from this earth, the world would return to chaos and to nothingness.

It is no wonder Psalm 24:1 says: "The earth is the Lord's, and the fulness thereof." This is a confession that the earth belongs to Him, that He and He alone has the right to reign, to rule, and to govern the world. Only by that confession as a foundation can we have a proper view of ecology and the environment.

God creates, God cares for His creation, and God celebrates His creation day by day. The Bible is very specific about this. The Bible tells us that He feeds the birds. Matthew 6:26, NIV says: "Look at the birds of the air; they do not sow or reap or store away in barns, and yet your heavenly Father feeds them."

Our Lord Jesus tells us that our heavenly Father clothes the lilies of the fields. "See how the lilies of the field grow. They do not labor or spin. Yet I tell you that not even Solomon in all his splendor was dressed like one of these" (Matt. 6:28-29, NIV). The Bible tells us that God hears the cries of animals and feeds them. "The lions roar for their prey and seek their food from God. The sun rises, and they steal away; they return and lie down in their dens" (Psalm 104:21-22, NIV).

The God who cares for and controls creation celebrates His creation even by naming and numbering the stars. In Psalm 147:4, NIV "He determines the number of the stars and calls them each by name." When our Lord Jesus came to this earth, He spoke tenderly and lovingly of God's creation. He often illustrated great spiritual truths by pointing to nature. He spoke of mustard seeds and mountains; He spoke of vineyards and trees; He performed miracles of nature, controlling the fish as well as the fowl, the winds and the seas.

In other words, God is immersed in His creation. This is the doctrine of immanence that God is present today, that God is real in His creation today. God rejoices in His creation. He is not the impersonal god of the deists or the idolatrous god of the pagans or the insipid god of the pantheists. He is the God of creation who cares. And we must learn to care as well.

We should look at our responsibility as Christians in the care of creation. In Revelation 4, John the beloved, the apostle, the prisoner of Patmos, tells how he was translated into the very presence of the throne room of God Almighty. There he saw mysterious wonders and visions and realities. In Revelation 4:6-11, NIV John records:

> In the center, around the throne, were four living creatures, and they were covered with eyes, in front and in back. The first living creature was like a lion, the second was like an ox, the third had a face like a man, the fourth was like a flying eagle. Each of the four living creatures had six wings and was covered with eyes all around, even under his wings. Day and night they never stop saying: 'Holy, holy, holy is the Lord God Almighty, who was, and is, and is to come.' Whenever the living creatures give glory, honor and thanks to him who sits on the throne and who lives for ever and ever, the twenty-four elders fall down before him who sits on the throne, and worship him who lives forever and ever. They lay their crowns before the throne and say: 'You are worthy, our Lord and God, to receive glory and honor and power, for you created all things and by your will they were created and have their being.'

Responding to the Creator

How should the Christian respond to the Creator and to the creation that God made? I mention three ways in which we ought to respond:

First is adoration. All of creation—all that God has made—is a doxology of praise to God. The very character of God, the nature of God, is reflected in what He has made and is making because God is not stagnant. God is immanent in His design and in His creative process. Whether we look into the telescope and see the majestic galaxies or whether we look into the microscope and see the intricacies of God's design, we are peering through a window in which we see the hand of God.

Romans 1:20 tells us that since the creation of the world people can clearly see God's invisible qualities—His eternal power and divine nature. Verse 23 says people turn the creation of God into an object of worship which is idolatry. Nature worship is as old as human history and as new as today. Yet our worship in heaven, our worship throughout all eternity, will reflect not only upon God's redemptive act but also His creative act. Back to back in the Book of Revelation in chapter 4 and chapter 5 are two songs. One, in chapter 4, is a creation song. Chapter 5 is a redemption song concerning the blood of the Lamb. We never can recognize Jesus as our Redeemer until we recognize Him first as our Creator. We introduce people to the Redeemer when they first realize that He is their Maker and, therefore, owns all they possess.

God is great and too big for the whole universe to contain Him, yet small enough to live in our hearts. Again, I say, until we admit our need and our faith in a Creator, we can never come to know Him as Redeemer.

Creation hymns once bothered me. I thought creation hymns were for "liberals" and the like. How wrong I was when I dug deeper into the Bible and began to study the hymns! Look at the hymn, *This Is My Father's World*:

>This is my Father's world,
>And to my list'ning ears,
>All nature sings, and round me rings
>The music of the spheres.
>This is my Father's world,
>I rest me in the thought
>Of rocks and trees, of skies and seas;
>His hand the wonders wrought.
>This is my Father's world,
>The birds their carols raise;
>The morning light, the lily white
>Declare their Maker's praise.
>This is my Father's world,
>He shines in all that's fair;
>In the rustling grass I hear him pass,
>He speaks to me ev'rywhere.
>This is my Father's world,
>O let me ne'er forget
>That though the wrong seems oft so strong,

God is the Ruler yet.
This is my Father's world,
The battle is not done;
Jesus who died shall be satisfied,
And earth and heaven be one.[2]

This is our Father's world, but the battle is not yet done. We must be soldiers as well as stewards in the battle. In our public worship, we must give believers an opportunity to praise God, the Creator, and to teach people the truths that He is God of the earth, the seasons, the wonder, and the beauty. His creation is an opportunity for all of us to worship Him.

Our responsibility and our response as Christians to the creation first is one of adoration and worship and praise to the Creator.

Our second way to respond is in that of celebration. Adoration and celebration are both similar and different. When I speak of celebration, I speak of enjoying and exalting in the joys of life because of the beauty of the earth and the creation. The Lord, the Father Almighty, gives all good gifts. The world is God's good gift. We treasure it. We take pleasure in it. We cherish it. And yet many have lost the joy, the wonder, and the celebration of God's creation.

Small children often take a flower and examine it petal by petal. I remember lying on a pallet in our backyard at our home on the east side of Fort Worth and looking up into the sky and being amazed at the shooting stars. As a child I delighted in the wonder of it all. It has been a long time since I have done that. It has been a long time since I have taken time to examine the beauty of a rose.

But in Christ, the wonder is even greater. Christ offers new life. That's what I like about seeing people born into the family of God and coming into our church. They add the wonder of the celebration and excitement to the fellowship. When I became a Christian, the grass became greener, the air cleaner, the skies bluer, the trees taller, the oceans wider because from the perspective of new life in

Jesus Christ, everything is different. I now see things transformed through the eyes of grace and the eyes of God's glory.

Through music, through poetry, through prose, through art, through sculpture, we can capture the wonder and celebrate the glory of creation. Francis Schaeffer has spoken and written much about the need of a renaissance of Christian art that reflects the beauty of the glory of God to celebrate these things. When we celebrate the creation, it even produces scientific inquiry, the desire to know more about what God has made and to discover the wonders and to celebrate the joys of His creation.

So the celebration of creation inspires me to get up in the morning, to smell the fresh air, to live in the joys and the color and the fragrance. Jesus said, "I am come that they might have life, and that they might have it more abundantly" (John 10:10, KJV). Certainly to experience the abundant life is to enjoy what God has made.

Thirdly, we should approach God's creation with preservation. This is where we focus on our responsibility of stewardship, the care of creation. Too often Christians have abdicated their responsibility in this area. We err if we turn this issue over to those who deny the Creator. Those of us who know and love and serve our Creator must be involved.

In the beginning God gave us the assignment to keep the garden of Eden and to till it. The Lord put people in the garden and told them to work it and to take care of it (Gen. 2:15). He never has changed that charge. Genesis 1:27-30 magnified that responsibility. In the garden when man and woman sinned, they became abusers of the earth and manipulators of what God had made. Isn't it interesting that the first sin concerned the breaking of God's command regarding the fruit of a tree? With this sin—with this rebellion—the earth was cursed. Because we are involved in the sin of Adam, because we are descended from Adam, we are also responsible for the pain and the suffering inflicted upon the earth. We also have as the new creation a responsibility to make restitution to the earth and to be involved in a healing ministry with what God has made.

We know our world is not going to be perfect until Jesus comes. We know we will not have peace until the Prince of Peace comes. And yet we strive, and we pray for peace. We know this world will not be perfect until the new creation, the real new world order, comes when Christ comes again. And yet, in the meanwhile, we must strive to preserve and to protect what God has made. Our goal is not perfecting the earth; our goal is protecting the earth. Jesus told us: "Occupy until I come." Literally, He meant, "Take care of business until I come." We know our first business is that of fulfilling the Great Commission, the charge to evangelize the world. In the overall scheme of things, certainly preaching the gospel is far more important than planting a tree, but I believe taking care of business includes taking care of God's earth.

In the Bible, creation and redemption are inseparable. The message of the Bible includes the physical as well as the spiritual, the temporal along with the eternal. When Jesus inaugurated the Lord's Supper, with the symbols of His body and of His blood, He took elements from nature—the bread and the fruit of the vine. The things God made symbolize our Lord's redemptive act.

And so, we are stewards with a message. I don't think our primary issue is Styrofoam cups. We are stewards with a message which includes creation and redemption; therefore, we send out farmers from our Foreign Mission Board; we send out agronomists now as well as preachers and teachers. This is one way our denomination, through our missionary enterprise, can be involved in the ecological and environmental issues.

The environment is a way—a bridge, a window—into the lives and hearts of people. Some 60 percent of Americans consider themselves environmentalists. That is a large group of people. Many of them are unbelievers, and some of them wonder why churches and Christians are not more involved with this subject.

Evangelism is a powerful environmental strategy. By that I

mean, fallen and sinful humanity destroys what God creates. Humanity without Jesus Christ is irresponsible because of its sin and need for salvation. People and nature are separated because of sin. Proverbs 12:10, NIV says: "A righteous man cares for the needs of his animal, but the kindest acts of the wicked are cruel." Only when people are restored in the second Adam can we return to the garden and till it with delight. Outside of Jesus Christ we become self-centered materialists and humanists, taking without giving. Greed and covetousness motivate us and dominate us.

Being told to have dominion over the earth does not mean we are to be the lords of the earth; we have only one Lord. It does not mean we are to go about the earth pillaging and torching the earth; we are to subdue the earth. To have dominion literally means to bring the earth under control for the sake of all of us, including the animal kingdom. It means not to conquer the earth but to care for and to cultivate the earth.

Stewardship and preservation include accepting a more simple life-style. Our world says, "More is better." The status quo pressures us to achieve and succeed. We seem never to be satisfied, never to be content. The Christian steward should learn contentment. How much is enough? How much comfort is enough? How much stuff is enough? This is important because the ways of greed destroy compassion. When we become greedy and self-centered, ignoring the deprived, ignoring the depressed, ignoring the devastation around us, we commit one of the most grievous sins of all. Jesus spoke of that rich man in hell who ignored the poor man day by day. Jesus spoke of that man who said, "I have so many crops, I have so much, I'm going to tear down my old barns and build newer barns and get myself in a hammock in the shade and sip lemonade and eat, drink, and be merry, for tomorrow I die." And God said, "Thou fool, this night thy soul shall be required of thee" (Luke 12:20, KJV). Total disregard brought that man to disaster.

The message is clear: Our undisciplined consumption must end. If we continue to gobble up our resources without regard to any stewardship and to spew out deadly waste over the land, the sea, the air, our city streets, our countryside, we well may be drawing the final curtain upon ourselves. Overconsumption cuts the heart out of compassion. It converts us to uncaring, unfeeling materialists and consumers. We no longer are sensitive to the great moral issues of our time. In a word, we have sinned against God by omitting our responsibility as wise stewards.

What One Person Can Do

Many of us wonder, "What can I do? I am only one person." How many times do we see in the Scripture how God called one person to make a difference? Claude Rhea, former president of Palm Beach Atlantic College, once spoke about touching the mere edge of a great need. I like that. We can't touch all needs, but we can touch the mere edge of a great need. We can become advocates. We have heard of consumer advocates. Where are the Christian advocates? We can become ambassadors with a message. We can volunteer in programs and missions that deal with this subject.

Mobberly Avenue Baptist Church in Longview, Texas, adopted several roads in its area. The congregation cares for and nurtures the area along those roads.

We can volunteer. We can influence public policy. In our Sunday School classes and from our pulpits we can teach the truths of stewardship. We can write letters to our representatives in Congress and to other public officials. We can pray. We can eliminate our own personal bad habits of overconsumption. We can simplify our life-styles. We can examine our own churches, our budgets, and our programs. We can establish a conservation group or committee in our churches. We can send missionaries who will care for creation. We can share our resources and pool our resources as did the church in Acts 2. All of this begins with repentance and faith. It means we are willing to accept our responsibility, to admit our failure and our sin, and to repent and by faith step forward.

We are stewards. The question is, "Are we good stewards or bad stewards?" We can become sensitive. We can refuse to live wastefully and carelessly. We can become informed. We can vote for sound environmental practices and officials who are committed to caring for the earth. We can make a difference. The question is, "Will we?"

Moses stood before the people and the land and said, "I have set before you life and death, blessing and cursing: therefore choose life" (Deut. 30:19, KJV). Will we choose life?

Notes

1. Francis A. Schaeffer, *Pollution and the Death of Man: The Christian View of Ecology* (Wheaton: Tyndale, 1970), 81.

2. *This Is My Father's World*, Words by Maltbie D. Babcock, 1901. Tune TERRA PATRIS, Franklin L. Sheppard, 1915.

10
Theology of Creation
Robert E. Naylor

Scriptures can assume faces. Some people have made a Scripture to live in your life by what you saw in their eyes, heard in their voices, felt in their lives. I have a friend who has been prominent in Baptist life. I have been with him in small circles when he was called on to pray. Always, without exception, when he prayed I listened and marveled. Gradually I began to realize that the following Scripture spoke to him:

> O Lord our Lord, how excellent is thy name in all the earth! who hast set thy glory above the heavens. Out of the mouth of babes and sucklings hast thou ordained strength because of thine enemies, that thou mightest still the enemy and the avenger. When I consider thy heavens, the work of thy fingers, the moon and the stars, which thou hast ordained; What is man, that thou art mindful of him? and the son of man, that thou visitest him? For thou has made him a little lower than the angels, and hast crowned him with glory and honour. Thou madest him to have dominion over the works of thy hands; thou hast put all things under his feet: All sheep and oxen, yea, and the beasts of the field; The fowl of the air, and the fish of the sea, and whatsoever passeth through the paths of the seas. O Lord our Lord, how excellent is thy name in all the earth! (Ps. 8, KJV)

The creation of God is good. It is good because it perfect. God makes it good in its concept, good in its motivation, and good in its activation. God made a perfect world. It is no wonder, then, that believer and unbeliever alike stand in awe, and often fear, of God's creation.

What does "good" mean? When we focus on a subject with which a friend agrees, that person will say, "Good, good." Those words don't mean a thing in the world unless you understand that friend and know and believe in him or her. In a certain kind of situation, another friend will say, "It is *very* good." I noticed recently that twice within a week I said, "This is good food." What do I mean by that word "good"?

The word "good" appears 346 times, with multiple inflections, all through the Old Testament. The Scripture says in Genesis that Abraham died in a good old age and says that Gideon died in a good old age. It even says of David that he died in a good old age. The Bible says God saw that which He had made, and it was good.

Deuteronomy often speaks of Israel as the good land. David said of Ahimaaz, "He is a good man" (2 Sam. 18:27, KJV). Acts 11:24, KJV describes Barnabas as "a good man and full of the Holy Ghost." The psalmist said, "A good man sheweth favour" (Ps. 112:5, KJV). Proverbs says, "A good man obtaineth favour of the Lord" (Prov. 12:2, KJV) and "A good man leaveth an inheritance" (Prov. 13:22, KJV). Solomon prayed, "That I may discern between good and evil" (1 Kings 3:9, RSV).

I love that passage in the New Testament, repeated in the Gospels, in which a young man comes running to Jesus. We call him the rich young ruler. He made his way through the crowd, fell at the feet of Jesus, and said, "Good Master, what shall I do that I may inherit eternal life? And Jesus said unto him, Why callest thou me good? there is none good but one, that is, God" (Mark 10:17-18, KJV).

God as Divine Spectator

What is "good" in creation? If you're describing this word "good" in terms of purpose, it means "well adapted, useful, profitable." Genesis 2:18, NIV says, "It is not good for the man to be alone." Let me suggest a point of interpretation that the good creation, the good environment, is the evaluation of God as the divine Spectator of all He has made.

For the Christian, the divine Spectator role offers no difficulty. How can God call the world into being and yet then observe it as One who is only present? Doesn't the psalmist say, "Thou has beset me behind and before, and laid thine hand upon me. Such knowledge is too wonderful for me; it is high, I cannot attain unto it." (Ps. 139:5-6, KJV). This omniscient, omnipresent, omnipotent God, who can act as a Spectator inside and outside His creation, looks on and says, "It is good."

Not only is God's creation good, but God reveals to us that He has set His glory upon the heavens. This is a plus for the believer. When studying the environment, Christians understand God indeed is in His creation. Look at God's creation as you would a crown. I have seen the crown jewels of emperors on display and could only marvel at their beauty. The Scripture tells how David's triumphant troops brought him the crown of a defeated king. David took the crown, which weighed 100 pounds, and put it upon his head. But a crown has never existed like that of creation.

When the Christian recognizes God's role in creation, he or she passes from awe to worship, from fear to reverence, from stillness to exultant praise, from the abstract wonder to the Person whom we adore. The Hebrew word for glory, *kabod*, speaks of heaviness, of weight. All of God presses a divine seal upon this world that He has made. Our Bible uses this word 200 times. It sometimes is translated beauty and sometimes translated majesty.

One group of the Psalms is called the Nature Psalms. One of these, Psalm 19, begins, "The heavens declare the glory of God; and the firmament sheweth his handiwork. Day unto day uttereth speech, and night unto night sheweth knowledge. There is no speech nor language, where their voice is not heard" (Ps. 19:1-3, KJV). These words led Haydn, in the last years of his life, to write, that magnificent composition, *The Heavens Are Telling*. You could pause a moment and listen to the voices and know the wonder of the presence of God.

Psalm 24 is the Sunday Psalm. It praises God as the sovereign Creator of this earth. Psalm 93 is the Friday Psalm. In the ancient Jewish worship it was the psalm always sung on that day. Psalm 93 has been called the "hymn of coronation." Psalm 104 is the creation hymn. It declares, "Thou art very great; thou art clothed with honour and majesty." It is interpreted splendor. The majesty of God incites this psalm. It has in it an exuberance, a youthful vigor, a divine movement as you consider the creation of God. Psalm 29 is the hymn of the storm.

A Personal Creation

The glory of the Lord, however, is not confined to the psalms. "And he Moses said, I beseech thee, shew me thy glory. . . . And He (God) said, Thou canst not see my face: for there shall no man see me, and live. . . . It shall come to pass, while my glory passeth by, that I will put thee in the cleft of the rock, and will cover thee with my hand while I pass by" (Ex. 33:18-22, KJV).

Chronicles says: "It came even to pass, as the trumpeters were as one . . . praising and thanking the Lord . . . For he is good; for his mercy endureth for ever: that then the house was filled with a cloud . . . So that the priests could not stand to minister . . . for the glory of the Lord had filled the house of God" (2 Chron. 5:13-14, KJV).

Ezekiel wrote: "The glory of the Lord came into the house," and "The glory of the Lord filled the house" (Ezek. 43:4-5, KJV).

Two people stand and look at a gorgeous sunset. It moves them to silence. One of them is a believer; one is not. The unbeliever stands in awe and sees the multihued wonder of a heaven so inflamed or stands and looks at a rainbow with its multitude of colors flung across the heavens and marvels. But the believer stands and looks upon the same beauty and turns unto Him whose name is Jehovah, who is the God of the storm and the God of the day and the God of the night, unto Him who bought us and redeemed us with a dear price. For one, it is wonder; for another it is worship. It is derivative.

The creation is personal, not impersonal. It is revealed in quality as well as in kind. In kind, it is good. In quality, it is personal and divine. The environment around us—our surroundings—reflects the presence of God. We are surrounded by God—not the pantheism which takes the inanimate and gives it life by one's concept of mind and an identity that is false. We perceive and receive the glory of God only by faith.

God not only created the environment; He created an environment. He made humans for fellowship with Him. They were to walk together in relationship. We humans are to live under the deity—as creatures God made in His likeness, capable of divine fellowship, responsible for the creation He gave us in stewardship. God says everything is very good. Literally, the Bible says creation is "to be good very." It was not simply good.

The environment, ecology, and our sins in this matter are not just somber subjects. We have a disposition to be "downbeat" about them. Remember the psalmist said, "The heavens declare the glory of God" (Ps. 19:1, KJV). This world, marred by man's disobedience and sin, still is an environment that speaks of God and reveals His glory. "Very good," He said. He was referring not to humankind alone but to the completed cosmos—with humankind as its crown and its glory.

Faith is purest in the life that keeps the context, saying, "Good, good, good." It is no wonder God forbids us to make graven images or any likeness. They can be described as the work of human beings and not worthy of worship. We should only worship the Creator.

When we focus on the environment, we are reminded that this creation is the very presence of God—God about us, as well as God in us.

The glory of creation reminds us that God cares for us. The psalmist said, "What is man that thou art mindful of him . . . that thou dost care for him?" (Ps. 8:4, RSV). No language is adequate to express the caring mind of God, who is both eternal and personal.

When you read the Psalms, you realize God not only is mindful of us, but He also visits us. 1 Peter 2:12, KJV says, "Glorify God in the day of visitation." God came to see me one day. I was not expecting Him. I didn't have things picked up in my life. I was not ready to receive a heavenly guest, but He came to a needy one and set it all in order.

And God comes to see you, too, in the midst of your tears or your trials or your perplexity or your frustrations with a sense of duty or the trial that seems to be always upon you, and suddenly the storm is stilled, and you sit and visit a while. You discover that the fullness of God has been placed on your life. "That thou art mindful of him . . . that thou visiteth him" (Heb. 2:6, KJV).

Scripture further tells us that God crowns His created individuals with the same glory that is in Him. "Thou hast made him a little lower than the angels, and hast crowned him with glory and honour" (Ps. 8:5, KJV). This means value—the magnitude of potential.

If we moved to address the hurt and the ill of this physical universe that is the handiwork of a personal God, I wonder if we have any idea of the potential for achievement that lies within our grasp. Most of us do not expect the miracles of God. We are a minority. We always have been a minority. We are outnumbered in the universe. And yet here is a minority that in God is a majority.

Saved Individuals Must Give Account

God also has given people dominion over all that He has made. God is in charge. If you think the universe is in chaos, think again. The universe is like a committee, and you are the chairperson. You are in charge. God tells us that we humans are in charge. God made us to have dominion over all that He has created. We are His stewards.

The Psalms say that all animals—domestic and wild, as well as fish and fowl—are under the dominion of the human race which

God has made and into whose hands God has entrusted His creation.

Nothing is left out. All of this universe is to be under humanity's dominion and humanity's responsibility. A saved individual is even more responsible and, therefore, must give an account. All things are under his dominion, and suddenly it becomes not just a nature hymn; it is a messianic hymn. Isn't that the end of the matter? He shall be Lord of Lords and King of Kings and His name shall be "above every name" (Phil. 2:9, KJV) and "every knee shall bow . . . and every tongue shall confess" (Rom. 14:11, KJV) and the ultimate dominion is the Lord's. The glory confounds us, floors us, exalts us, demands of us, imbues us. Glory! Glory! Glory!

V
The Practical Application

11

Environmental Issues in the U.S. and Around the World

T. Rick Irvin

The principal topic among environmental issues receiving public attention in the 1970s and 1980s has been the discharge and distribution of hazardous/waste chemicals into the environment. These have ranged from agricultural chemicals to industrial pollutants to toxicants that naturally occur in the food supply. The public has been concerned about how exposure to toxic chemicals affects humans and the environment. This concern has produced increasing regulatory constraints on the manufacture and use of various classes of chemical agents.

The cost of monitoring natural toxins in the environment, as well as the cost of monitoring and remediating accidental discharges of human-produced chemicals, absorbs billions of dollars each year from the world economy. In this chapter we will look at some current and future environmental concerns about hazardous/waste chemicals in the environment.

Hazardous Wastes at Industry Sites

National attention has been focused on the health and environmental hazards associated with exposure to the large quantity of toxic waste chemicals produced by past as well as current manufacturing industries. Recent surveys of hazardous waste generation sites have reported more than 14,000 installations generating wastes regulated by the current Resource Conservation and Recovery Act (RCRA) and more than 5,000 facilities treating, storing, or disposing of hazardous wastes under RCRA-regulating controls.[1] Tabulation of waste mixtures generated at these sites indicates more than 80 billion gallons (297 million metric tons) of hazardous waste being generated on an annual basis.

How much toxic waste remediation costs the federal government is especially noteworthy. Current estimates target federal expenditures at more than 300 million dollars to clean up just 80 U.S. waste sites, leaving more than 10,000 remaining U.S. hazardous waste sites for future attention.

With the development of many new technologies that are heralded as new sources of U.S. industrial growth toward the year 2000, people are beginning to realize that serious toxic waste storage and disposal problems will accompany this growth.[2] These new industrial wastes include: (1) toxic solvents employed in semiconductor manufacturing (e.g., trichloroethylene, trichloroethane); (2) toxic specialty chemicals produced in support of electronics and fiber optics manufacture (glycol ethers, hydrazines, etc); (3) toxic solvents for recovery of recombinant DNA-derived pharmaceuticals (chloroform, hexanes); and (4) toxic waste salts derived from high technology gasses (arsines, phosgenes, diboranes).

Furthermore, current technologies for hazardous waste site prioritization do not address a principal, emerging source of human health hazard derived from leaking hazardous storage facilities—contamination of surface and groundwater supplies. Recent revelations regarding groundwater quality near semiconductor manufacturing facilities in Silicon Valley, California, illustrate the coordinate water quality problems potentially caused by continued improper storage of waste chemical products.[3] Repeated incidences of water source contamination in the Silicon Valley area by industrial solvents engendered the Underground Chemical Waste Tank Analysis by the state of California in which 80 hazardous waste test sites were routinely monitored for waste chemical leakage.

Of these sites, 64 (80 percent) indicated subsurface contamination of soil or groundwater, and 57 (70 percent) indicated immediate hazard of drinking water contamination. Toxic contaminants identified in these monitoring studies included solvents, acids, toxic metals, resins, and fuels that had leaked from product and raw material storage tanks, waste chemical tanks, fuel tanks, and piping systems. Rapid, qualitative spot checks of stored tanks at other semiconductor manufacturing plants throughout the country confirmed similar water contamination problems elsewhere.

In the future, people concerned about remedying hazardous wastes not only will be concerned about leaking waste at past sites but also about poorly regulated hazardous waste holding sites from emerging industries.

Defense Industry Wastes

Recent national attention has been focused on the environmental and human health hazards associated with toxic chemical and nuclear wastes stored at Department of Energy (DOE) facilities around the U.S. These facilities include the Rocky Flats Site in Colorado, the Hanford Reservation in Washington State, and the Savannah River Site on the Georgia/South Carolina border. Recent surveys of hazardous wastes stored or released at these sites have reported environmental and safety problems at 17 major DOE weapons plants and 83 additional DOE sites involved in processing nuclear material. Tabulation of nuclear and chemical wastes produced at these sites over the past 30 to 40 years indicates a wide spectrum of chemical and nuclear hazardous wastes are presently stored at DOE sites.[4] For example:

1. Fernald Materials Production Center, Fernald, Ohio: Currently maintains concrete silos holding more than 200,000 cubic feet of uranium refining tailings (contaminated with significant quantities of radium-226) and fly ash piles holding over 50,000 tons of natural uranium-contaminated material.

2. Savannah River Site, Aiken, South Carolina: Has generated more than 6.5 million cubic feet of high-level, radioactively contaminated liquid waste and currently serves as the final burial ground for tons of radioactively contaminated solid wastes from other DOE facilities around the country.

Evidence that the DOE has a growing concern about how much

hazardous waste is stored at national sites is apparent in the exponential growth in federal expenditures recommended for toxic waste remediation. DOE and industry estimates indicate that just to characterize and assess inactive DOE sites will cost 13 to 15 billion dollars. Final costs for remedying current wastes at operating facilities are conservatively estimated to be 50 billion dollars.

Estimates factoring long-term effects of DOE site contaminants are more than 400 billion dollars. These figures do not include costs to properly contain and treat radioactive contaminants derived from future nuclear processing activity.

People are beginning to realize that a wide diversity of chemical, nuclear, and mixed hazardous wastes currently populate DOE facilities. This fact is sharpening public debate on remedial hazardous waste disposal issues at national DOE facilities.

This wide diversity of wastes includes:

1. Radionuclides (uranium, plutonium, strontium, cesium);
2. Metals (chromium, mercury, lead, arsenic, cadmium);
3. Volatile Organic Agents (trichloroethylene, carbon tetrachloride);
4. Nonvolatile Organic Agents (PCB's, organophosphate and chlorinated hydrocarbon pesticides); and
5. Polycyclic Aromatic Hydrocarbons (derived from coal and fly ash: benzo(a)pyrene, fluoranthene, phenanthrene).

The Department of Energy's concern about the future safe operation of nuclear processing sites also has stemmed from the agency's recent recognition that improperly managed hazardous chemical wastes now may pose an additional, emerging source of human health concern—contamination of groundwater and surface water supplies. Recent reports of inadequate hazardous chemical storage facilities at DOE sites have engendered extensive chemical monitoring programs at many of the nation's sites.

Chemical analyses of groundwater and surface sampling stations at the Savannah River Site, for example, have recorded concentrations of toxic and cancer-causing organic solvents (trichloroethylene and perchloroethylene) as high as 200 parts per million.

Similar chemical analyses of sediments near coal ash storage basins have reported contamination by cancer-causing polycyclic aromatic hydrocarbons. These include phenanthrene, fluoranthene, and benzo(a)pyrene. Rapid, qualitative spot checks of DOE sites around the country have confirmed similar water and sediment contamination problems elsewhere. The fact that managing some of these wastes, such as coal fly ash, has not significantly changed in recent years, causes added concern.

Waste Problems of a High-Tech Industry

The semiconductor industry has enjoyed one of the best reputations for environmental cleanliness of all general manufacturing industries. Municipalities, industrial organizations, and environmental groups have, in the past, envisioned microelectronics as an "environmentally benign" industry important to struggling economies. Absent are the sooty smokestacks and noxious-smelling waste streams characteristic of traditional "rust belt" steel and manufacturing industries.

Personnel, dressed in special clothing, work within near-sterile production facilities. Because the smallest speck of dust can flaw a semiconductor wafer, dust levels within semiconductor operations are kept at levels much lower than within modern hospitals. Both air and water supplies supporting chip production rooms are strictly monitored to prevent accidental particulate or bacterial contamination.

The absence of obvious health threats has supported a unique aspect of the microelectronics industry: The work force maintains one of the highest percentages of women among all sectors of manufacturing. Microelectronics workers do not face obvious health threats such as asbestos exposure or machinery operating at high temperatures. Much like conventional electronics industries, governmental agencies envisioned microelectronics production lines of well-paid workers seated at work stations quietly soldering wires to printed circuit boards.

The rapid growth of semiconductor technology in the United States has fostered proliferation of direct production facilities as well as support industries. Overnight, regions of the U.S. have become synonymous with high-tech manufacturing: Silicon Valley near San Francisco and Route 128 around Boston. The state of Texas recently has become an active participant and benefactor in the growth and research advances within the semiconductor industry.

Events in Silicon Valley during 1981, however, have drastically altered governmental and public opinions about the environmental safety of the semiconductor industry. Leaks were discovered in storage tanks at the Fairchild Semiconductor Corporation plant. Organic solvents used to manufacture semiconductor components were found seeping through the soil and into the surrounding aquifers and drinking water wells in nearby San Jose. An underground fiberglass tank at the Fairchild facility leaked an estimated 58,000 gallons of solvents before it was identified. More than 267 plaintiffs already have brought multimillion dollar lawsuits against the company and other defendants. These suits charge that deaths and a number of medical problems—birth defects, skin disorders, and cancer—have resulted from groundwater pollution in this area.

As mentioned above, follow-up studies by the California Regional Water Quality Control Board initiated an underground tank leak detection program through which 80 test sites were routinely monitored for toxic chemical contamination. Of these sites, 64 (80 percent) indicated subsurface contamination of soils and groundwater, and 57 (70 percent) indicated an immediate hazard of drinking water contamination. Toxic contaminants identified included solvents, acids, toxic metals, resins, and fuels that leaked from product and raw material storage tanks, water chemical tanks, fuel tanks, and piping systems. Rapid spot checks of storage tanks at other semiconductor manufacturing plants throughout the country confirmed similar water contamination and problems at other locations.

Examination of chemicals used in semiconductor chip manufacturing during the early 1980s illustrates numerous sources of surface and groundwater contamination surrounding high densities of semiconductor plants. During the first phase of chip manufacturing, a purified silicon ingot is produced by crystallizing wafers which are first cleaned in baths of acids and hydrocarbon solvents. These wafers then are heated in a high-oxygen atmosphere to create a nonconductive silicon-dioxide insulating film on the wafer's surface. Stage two of chip production involves baking a semiconductor grid onto the surface of the wafer. This uses a process similar to photolithography in printing. This "acid-etched" wafer with its imprinted circuit pattern finally is impregnated with dopants which create regions of positive and negative charge on the chip's surface—regions that form the transistors or active circuits that process electrical signals.

A closer examination of this process finds that numerous hazardous and toxic chemicals are used in various stages of semiconductor chip manufacturing. These chemicals end up as waste byproducts. Common solvents used in washing stages, such as trichloroethylene, are considered suspect cancer-causing agents to animals and human beings. Trichloroethylene is one of the principal groundwater pollutants associated with concentrations of semiconductor manufacturing facilities. Glycol ethers, such as 2-ethoxyethanol and 2-methoxyethanol, are considered suspect toxicants to the human reproductive system. Birth defects, prenatal toxicity, and impaired sperm development have been reported in laboratory animal studies. Dopant gases used to alter conductivity of semiconductor crystal materials include arsine, phosgene, and diborane gases. Arsenic, when converted to arsenic trioxide, is very toxic to human beings. (Increased rates of lung, bronchus, and lymph gland cancer previously have been reported among workers within industries where large quantities of arsenic are present.) The semiconductor industry, much like the petrochemical, agrichemical, and metallurgical industries, provides a complete spectrum of potential pollution problems. Anyone of those problems, upon uncontrolled or unchecked environmental discharge, could severely impact an area's health and economic well-being.

An Emerging Area of Hazardous Wastes

The Resource Conservation and Recovery Act of 1976 (RCRA) regulates transporting and disposing of hazardous materials. Under RCRA, the owners of hazardous materials (e.g., used dry cleaning fluid, spent batteries, out-of-date pesticides) must maintain records following hazardous material during transport to EPA-approved disposal sites. EPA itself establishes the list of materials regulated under RCRA and approves waste disposal sites.

RCRA was designed with two primary purposes.[5] The first was to save energy by identifying sources of waste materials which could be recycled. The second was to ensure that hazardous materials, especially toxic chemicals, were properly disposed. Previously toxic waste chemicals commonly were disposed of (in a clandestine manner) instead of being transported to an EPA-approved site.

Under Section 301(b)(2)(A) of the 1980 Amendments to RCRA, Congress temporarily exempted several types of solid wastes from regulation as hazardous wastes pending further study by the EPA.[6] Among the categories of wastes exempted were: "drilling fluids, produced waters, and other wastes associated with the exploration, development, or production of crude oil or natural gas."

The scientific support or rationale for this exemption derived from the fact that oil and gas wastes fall within a general category of wastes that RCRA regarded as "special" because:

1. their unusually high volume makes the application of some RCRA regulatory requirements technically infeasible or impractical, and

2. their relatively low level of apparent environmental hazard (based on data available in 1980).

Congress' intent in temporarily exempting these wastes from RCRA regulation was to provide an opportunity to develop an appropriate strategy for their management should new or additional measures prove to be needed.

The current statutory exemption of oil and gas drilling wastes originated in EPA's proposed hazardous waste regulations of December 8, 1978 (43 FR 58946). Proposed 40 CFR 2350.46 contained standards for "special wastes" which reduced requirements for several types of wastes produced in large volume and that EPA believed may be lower in toxicity than other wastes regulated as hazardous wastes under RCRA. One of these categories of special wastes was "gas and oil drilling muds and oil production brines." The test of whether a particular waste qualifies under the exemption of "special wastes" can be made in relation to the following three separate criteria:

1. Exempt wastes must be associated with measures

a. to locate oil or gas deposits,

b. to remove oil or natural gas from the ground, or

c. to remove impurities from such substances, provided that the purification process is an integral part of primary field operations.

2. Only waste streams intrinsic to the exploration for, or the development and production of, crude oil or natural gas are subject to exemption. Waste streams generated at oil or gas facilities that are not uniquely associated with the exploration, development, or production activities are not exempt. (Examples of these later classes would include spent solvents from equipment cleanup, or air emissions from diesel engines used to operate drilling rigs.)

3. Drilling fluids, produced waters, and other wastes intrinsically derived from primary field operations associated with the exploration, development or production of crude oil, natural gas, or geothermal energy are subject to exemption. Primary field operations encompass production-related activities but not transportation or manufacturing activities. With respect to oil production, primary field operations encompass those activities usually occurring at or near the wellhead, but prior to the transfer of oil from an

individual field facility or a centrally located facility to a carrier (e.g., pipeline or trucking concern).

During the previous four years, EPA twice has proposed to classify oil and gas drilling wastes as hazardous materials requiring disposal according to RCRA guidelines. Some chemicals generated as by-products of oil and gas production, as well as some components of crude oil itself, have been shown to elicit acute and chronic human disease and ecological damage. Currently, approximately 50 million barrels of produced water are generated per day in the U.S. at the rate of 8 barrels of water produced for each barrel of oil. Since approximately 70 percent of U.S. wells produce approximately two to three barrels of oil per day, regulation of by-product waters at the site proves difficult.

The Regulation Dilemma

Previous scientific findings supporting federal and state review of the regulatory status of oil and gas drilling wastes have come from chemical evaluations of these wastes. Variations in the chemical composition of drilling wastes are known to exist from samples collected in different parts of the U.S., as well as in different parts of the world; however, key classes of toxic constituents of oil and gas drilling wastes have been identified at multiple locations. These include:

a. toxic metals (beryllium, cadmium, chromium, arsenic)

b. radionuclides (radium, cesium, uranium, thorium)

c. monocyclic and polycyclic aromatic hydrocarbon carcinogens (naphtha lene, fluoranthene, benzo(a)pyrene, benzene)

Equally important, these contaminants have been documented as toxic constituents in shellfish collected from areas into which produced waters have been discharged. Recent studies funded by the Environmental Protection Agency concluded that radiological and hydrocarbon data from the *in situ* experiments clearly demonstrated that oysters growing near produced water outfalls can accumulate radium 226, volatile aromatics and polynuclear aromatic hydrocarbons in soft tissues within a relatively short period of time.[7]

These reports have added additional fuel to arguments that, because of ecological environmental and toxicological effects, oil and gas drilling wastes should be regulated as toxic/hazardous wastes. Chief among the areas most actively debating the need to increasingly regulate oil and gas drilling wastes is the Louisiana-Texas Gulf Coast. Because of the fact that much of the oil and gas drilling activity in these states occurs in coastal areas, questions about the human and environmental impact of trace contaminants in these wastes are exacerbated by the potential for distant transport by surface waters and contamination of economically important food fish domains.

Reregulation of oil and gas drilling wastes as RCRA-regulated hazardous wastes as proposed by EPA would eliminate the application of virtually all conventional removal and treatment technologies for disposing oil and gas drilling wastes. Technologies such as landfarming and open-pit disposal would be eliminated or tightly restricted so as not to be economically feasible. Offsite-treatment would fulfill currently envisioned requirements by EPA, but only a small number of firms currently exist to perform offsite treatment, clearly insufficient to support even current gas and oil industry needs. Recirculation of these wastes will solve some of the problems and certainly will reduce the overall volume of waste. However, small oil and gas firms will not be able to afford the systems needed for recycling and recirculation of wastes; further, this method does not address the problems of disposal of produced waters. Clearly reregulation of oil and gas drilling wastes as hazardous waste would:

a. greatly increase the costs of oil and gas drilling;

b. shift oil and gas exploration from the U.S. to overseas locations; and

c. greatly exacerbate the problem of hazardous materials disposal which already exists in the U.S.

EPA is focusing attention to oil and gas drilling wastes with the object of determining if some of these materials should be brought under RCRA control within the next two to three years. These wastes have been documented to contain toxic chemicals known to cause human disease, and the volume of waste produced at drilling sites is substantial. Litigation by environmental groups concerning the disposal of these volumes of toxic metals and radioactivity will force some regulatory constraint of current practices. Many questions, however, still are under active debate. These questions include:

a. how much oil and gas drilling waste should be classified as hazardous material and

b. what method(s) will be approved for drilling waste disposal.

The U.S. does not have adequate facilities to properly store current volumes of RCRA-regulated, hazardous industrial wastes; thus, facilities are not available to accommodate the large volume of drilling wastes these proposals would regulate. American Petroleum Institute sources indicate that if oil and gas drilling wastes were regulated overnight as hazardous waste material, the cost to the oil and gas industry would approach 40 billion dollars per year. Currently, few commercial firms have the facilities in place, parallel to that developed for the management of hazardous waste chemicals from the synthetic chemical industry, for the management and disposal of oil and gas drilling waste regulated as hazardous materials.

Potential Human Health Hazards

A main reason for focusing public attention on the ways in which humans are exposed to hazardous waste/chemicals in the environment is the realization that, upon direct human contact, some toxic agents contained within the complex mixtures of environmental pollutants may elicit human disease. Many human diseases responsible for significant percentages of human death and hospitalization have been shown to have genetic, nutritional, microbial, and viral etiologies. However, for many important human diseases, naturally occurring and man-made chemicals also have been shown to be potential causative factors along with those listed above. Human diseases for which some chemical agent has been demonstrated as an etiological agent include:

- cancer
- birth defects
- neurological disease
- immunological disease
- diseases of the neurosensory system
- dermatological diseases
- reproductive dysfunction in men and women

Evidence supporting concern about uncontrolled human exposure to toxic chemicals in the environment has come from many sources. Examples of this evidence for several categories of human disease are as follows.

Birth Defects and Prenatal Toxicity

Exposure of preborn babies to prenatal toxins and teratogens has been identified as an important causative factor of the 200,000 birth defects and over 560,000 spontaneous abortions, miscarriages and stillbirths observed annually in the United States. Of these birth defects and conceptus/neonate deaths, epidemiological studies indicate 25 percent have underlying genetic causes while 10 to 15 percent are directly associated with exposure to:

- radiation (e.g., x-rays)
- viruses (e.g,. rubella or German measles)
- drugs (e.g., thalidomide)

The remaining 65 percent previously have been ascribed to unknown factors. Increasing reports of human prenatal toxicity caused by overt and chronic chemicals exposure have implicated toxic environmental compounds as important causative agents of human prenatal toxicity unaccounted for by other factors. Previous concerns about prenatal toxic hazards from hazardous waste site toxins have principally centered on toxic organic solvents (trichloroethylene) and halogenated polycyclic hydrocarbons (chlorinated pesticides, dioxins). However, reports of prenatal mortality and teratogenesis in laboratory animals induced by mixtures common to hazardous waste sites (such as creosote as well as spent petroleum distillate mixtures) strongly support the need for more vigorous assessment of prenatal health effects elicited by hazardous waste site-associated compounds.

Neurological Disease

Experts have recognized the widespread occurrence of acute as well as chronic neurotoxicity among people who continuously are exposed to environmental agents. This fact has focused attention recently on both how little detailed information we have to identify nervous system toxins as well as how little information we have on those chemical and biochemical properties characterizing compounds which damage nerve tissues.

Recent reports of lead-induced neurotoxicity and developmental abnormalities in urban children undergoing chronic lead exposure from gasoline and paint have heightened public attention about the capacity of environmental toxins, known to cause more well-known diseases such as cancer and reproductive dysfunction, to also cause neurotoxic effects. Further reports of chronic neurotoxicity observed in workers exposed to kepone, aliphatic solvents, and plasticizers have expanded environmental health concerns about chemically mediated nervous system effects of chemical classes commonly found as groundwater pollutants as well as hazardous waste components.

Reproductive Toxicity

Exposure to environmental chemicals increasingly has been implicated as a major causative factor in the high rates of spontaneous abortion and miscarriage observed in the U.S. Reports of female reproductive capacity during the 1970s and 1980s indicate that more than 560,000 infant deaths, spontaneous abortions, stillbirths, and miscarriages are recorded each year because of defective fetal development. More recent studies suggest this figure may underrepresent the actual incidence of spontaneous abortions and miscarriages by a factor of 2 or 3 since many women during the first weeks of pregnancy do not realize they have sustained a pregnancy loss. As in the case of prenatal toxicity and birth defects, epidemiological studies indicate that roughly 70 percent of reported cases of spontaneous abortion and miscarriage are ascribed to unknown etiological factors. Further, recent analyses of health effects reported by human populations residing near leaking hazardous waste sites have reported reproductive dysfunction in women as one of the predominant health impairments recorded.

Advances and Successes

In listing past and current environmental concerns in the above sections, one might conclude that our management of the environment has not yielded any successes nor has it evidenced any improvement. Nothing could be farther from the truth. The fact that these environmental problems have been so well characterized and evaluated alone suggests that governmental agencies and industrial organizations have grown more acutely sensitive to environmental management. Further, the birth and growth of joint government-industry-academic organizations to seek causes of environmental problems as well as cost-effective solutions portends a bright future for proactive evaluation of the potential environmental impacts of industrial and agricultural activities.

Intensive studies by governmental, industrial, and academic groups have yielded new technologies with which to more quickly and more accurately evaluate and remediate environmental damage from hazardous/waste chemical discharge. Listed below are two success stories in the development of new tools for better management of the environment.

Development of New Tools

Hazardous complex chemical mixtures of primary human health concern in the U.S.—sludges, wood-preserving wastes, combustion soots, and dioxin-contaminated soils—contain numerous components (10 to 150 components) within complex matrices. Analyzing these toxic components of complex mixtures involves using time-expensive protocols that include, at a minimum, the following steps: extraction of waste samples, chemical fractionation of the extracts, and identification of the separated chemicals by expensive instrumentation methods.

Nagging doubts about method efficiency and sample contamination often plague these protocols. Current methods for assessing chemical ingredients within isolated toxic complex mixtures as well as contaminated surrounding environments (air, soil, and water) also depend, by-and-large, on lengthy, extensive chemical identification of all chemical classes present. This is followed by assignment to toxic hazards associated with those chemicals which are present. Traditional analytical methods for chemical identification, including gas and high-pressure liquid chromatography as well as mass spectrometry, are not currently feasible for rapid, routine analysis of complex chemical mixtures. This is due to nagging questions about the loss of quantitatively minor mixture components as well as the recovery of mixture components. Multiple analyses must be performed for both identification and quantitation of chemical classes in complex environmental mixtures. Proper identification of even specific classes requires preliminary information on the types of chemicals to be analyzed, preliminary information which would require even additional analytical tasks.

Further, most current methods for chemical analysis of environmental samples contaminated by toxic chemical agents require weeks or months for results at commercial costs of thousands of dollars. One new technology assisting in the improved measurement and management of environmental problems is the development of field-deployable chemical instrumentation permitting the identification and measurement of toxic chemical agents within a one- to two-hour time frame at the site of generation or storage. Two such technologies developed in recent years which are significantly impacting the improved management of hazardous/waste chemical sites are:

1. "Microchip Gas Chromatograph" for determining volatile toxic chemicals in hazardous waste sites.

Microchip gas chromatograph technology is based on the fabrication and construction of key chemical instrumentation components into a silicon wafer. The microchip GC instrument, no larger than a credit card, can rapidly detect (one to five minutes) volatile toxic chemicals released from hazardous waste sites and waste-amended materials (air, water, soil).

2. "Thermal Chromatography" for determining nonvolatile compounds in hazardous wastes.

Thermal chromatography technology is based on the thermal elution and chromatographic separation of toxic chemicals in solid or semi-solid materials (e.g., rock, soil, plastics). The thermal chromatograph, which is currently being operated at hazardous waste sites undergoing remediation, can rapidly (in 90 minutes) identify and measure toxic chemicals from complex solid or semi-solid matrices without the need for any sample preparation or extraction.

Monitoring Human Health Effects

A viable adjunct technology complementary to chemical analysis of toxic chemical mixtures is the direct assessment of toxic effects associated with mixture isolates. Prioritizing toxic chemical mixtures as well as individual mixture ingredients according to human toxic effects would focus public attention to those mixtures of greatest public health risk. Complex mixtures containing small quantities of toxic chemicals or large quantities of relatively nontoxic agents would be given a lower priority than would mixtures with high quantities of toxic agents or critical mixtures of chemicals which interact (synergize) to potentiate toxic effects of individual chemical species.

Whole animal experiments to characterize the toxic effects of hazardous wastes, however, prove too costly and lengthy to be of adequate use to properly indicate toxic potential. Whole animal toxicity studies of mixture isolates also preclude the accurate assessment of potential interactive properties of toxic chemical components. Short-term test systems are needed which can predict the relative toxicity of toxic complex chemical mixtures as well as the mixture itself. Such short-term tests, monitoring the predominant human health effects of waste constituents, would indicate waste sites which need the most attention.

Recently new toxicity test systems have been developed which rapidly identify and evaluate the toxic constituents of hazardous waste chemicals. Developing these test systems is based on the application of novel human and animal cell systems which permit analysis of toxic chemicals for four human and animal toxic effects. These cell culture systems permit the rapid assessment, monitoring, and prioritizing of hazardous waste as well as prediction of the toxic potential of complex hazardous waste mixtures isolated from various environmental samples. These toxicity tests, which can be conducted at a suspect hazardous waste site, have been used to evaluate the toxic potency of hazardous wastes. Successful application of these toxicity tests for the management of hazardous waste sites include:

1. assessment of the human hazards of hazardous wastes;

2. identification and evaluation of the toxic ingredients in hazardous waste sites;

3. prioritization of hazardous waste sites for remediation based on imminent human health risk; and

4. design of waste management technologies to more rapidly remediate hazardous waste sites.

The prevalence of all these documented environmental/health hazards today poses serious questions about how and when we act to protect ourselves and our environment from the onslaught besieging our world today.

Notes

1. U.S. Environmental Protection Agency, *National Survey of Hazardous Waste Generators and Treatment, Storage and Disposal Facilities Regulated Under RCRA in 1981 (US Government Printing Office*, 1984 0-442-790.

2. T. R. Irvin, Proceedings of the Conference: *Texas Water Resource Issues Towards the Twenty First Century.* Texas Water Resources Institute, 1987.

3. J. LaDou, Technology Review 18 (1984) 647.

4. Department of Energy *1990 Research, Development, Deployment, Testing, and Evaluation Program for DOE Waste Sites.*

5. Congressional Budget Office, *Federal Liabilities Under Hazardous Waste Laws.* CBO Office, May, 1990.

6. Environmental Protection Agency. *Report to Congress: Management of Wastes from the Exploration, Development, and Production of Crude Oil, Natural Gas, and Geothermal Energy,* EPA/530-5W-88-003, 1988.

7. *Environmental Distribution of By-products from Petroleum Exploration*, Report to the Environmental Protection Agency and the Louisiana Marine Consortium, 1990.

12

How to Deal with the Media on Ecological Issues

Louis A. Moore

In the 1960s, a Canadian communications professor named Marshall McLuhan took assorted and related facts that many people knew but did not fully comprehend and put them together in a wider context with a revolutionary perspective.

McLuhan noted how the development of marvelous new inventions had magnified dramatically the ability of humans to communicate with each another in recent decades. McLuhan puzzled over the large and assorted number of messages that each person in the new era receives via newspaper, radio, television, movie theaters, stereos, and so forth. He wondered what such an unprecedented barrage of images and messages was doing to people's minds. He was the first person to ask in a major way—pointedly and loudly—what introducing the tools of the mass media meant to people individually and to civilization as a whole.

He concluded that the media was "reshaping and restructuring patterns of social interdependence and every aspect of personal life."[1]

McLuhan's illustration for what was happening became a catchword for tens of thousands of students of communication during the 1960s. After those of us who were students in the tumultuous 1960s read McLuhan's famous *The Medium is the Massage*, we realized we live in a "global village" in which our neighbors are as close as the next continent—our world as emotionally linked as if we lived next door to an Alpine village or an African mud hut.

Starting the Revolution: The Printing Press

Four hundred years before McLuhan, the revolution he pinpointed began. It started with the birth of the world's first printing press.

Before Gutenberg's new printing press, people communicated with each other in mostly individual ways—by word of mouth or through handwritten letters. Before Gutenberg, books were handwritten. Thus the total number of volumes produced was tiny by today's standards. For centuries the Bible itself had to be painstakingly copied by hand—letter for letter, word for word—often by monks in secluded monasteries.

Gutenberg's press was like the "shot heard around the world" in the American revolution. With his marvelous invention, Gutenberg reproduced literary works with astonishing speed and conformity. But compared to today's standards, Gutenberg's press was an anguishingly slow process producing only a limited number of copies.

In its 400 years, the printing press has undergone major changes that have improved its speed, efficiency, reproduction capabilities, and cost. In the past 20 years, printing has undergone giant leaps forward. Major improvements have added color to the dull gray pages of newsprint and made the focus sharper while reducing the per-unit cost. It is not hyperbole to say that everything I learned just 25 years ago in my college journalism classes now is obsolete, thanks to the linking of computers to printing presses and the introduction of "cold type" and desk-top publishing and its laser printers.

On the world's stage, newspapers themselves are relatively new inventions. Although it is difficult to comprehend, newpapers before the 1830s were considered items for the elite rather than items for the masses. Only in this century have such publications as the *Wall Street Journal*, *New York Times*, and *Time* reached masscirculation figures. *Editor & Publisher* frets these days about the "recession" in the newspaper publishing business, which basically means the tremendous growth in the number of readers during the past three decades has slowed to a snail's pace. What often is missed in discussions about the slowdown in newspaper publishing is the fact that more people than ever have access to newspapers.

While the maturation of the printing press occurred, the birth and maturation of other forms of mass communication were under way simultaneously as well.

The first radio station in the United States was launched in 1919. Today, only 72 years later, media experts say we have two radios for every man, woman, boy, or girl living in this country. Radio rouses us from our beds in the mornings, acts as our companion when we drive our cars to work, entertains us when we relax at our homes, jogs with us, de-stresses us when we work in our offices, and even abruptly enters our lives when someone has put us on "hold" when we telephone them.

Thomas Edison invented the first phonograph in 1877. Electric phonographs went on sale for the first time to the public in 1925. And since then, more and more turntables have been spinning in more and more homes, offices, businesses, and places of entertainment. Even as it gives way to new dimensions in the form of cassette players and disc players, phonographs remain a key element in many of our lives. This medium spawned the recorded music industry which now is so large "it has developed a number of sub-specialty forms—hard rock, soft rock, acid rock, punk rock."[2]

Edison invented the first movie projector in 1893, but it was not until 1914 that movie studios began to blossom. Movies reached their zenith in 1946 when some 90 million Americans a week trekked to their local theaters. After declining, movies today are enjoying an unprecedented rebound, thanks to video recordings which make them available in homes at minimal costs or at theaters featuring a half dozen or more screens.

The first television was displayed at the New York City World's Fair in 1939, but television did not begin appearing in homes until

1946, shortly after World World II ended. Noted journalism professor Ronald T. Farrar has said, "To an astonishing degree, individuals and entire families organize their meals, their evenings, and their social engagements around the daily television program logs; their hurried conversations occur mostly during station breaks. Television's hold on contemporary society is powerful and pervasive, and shows no signs of becoming less so in the years ahead."[3]

How Audiences Respond

All this means that the past 100 years have witnessed a phenomenal growth in these new tools of human communication, most of which have been brought to maturity alongside one another during the past 50 years.

Marshall McLuhan looked at these marvelous new vehicles of human communication and saw the broader context. He asked what type of messages each of these forms of mass media was communicating. He asked how their audiences responded to each form of media. He then made his dramatic media-shattering pronouncement: "The medium is the massage."[4] That statement in 1967 set off a furious debate about whether newspapers, magazines, books, televisions, radios, movies, and other forms of the mass media report the world as it is or create a perspective about life that is self-perpetuating and biased.

Before McLuhan, few schools of journalism offered courses in communication theory. After McLuhan, theories of mass communication became the rage. This has happened to the extent that today a debate is under way between media operators and journalism professors over how much theory of mass communication is enough. The professors say more is needed; the media owners and operators say they have had it with graduates who can spout theory but can't spell or report and write a simple obituary. Whatever the final result of the debate, theories of mass communication are here to stay. They well should be, as each of us is massaged, manipulated, maneuvered, and informed by the media of our choice.

Politicians have picked up on certain limited aspects of McLuhan's theories and have emphasized the negative: They love to say the media is an elite fourth estate wreaking havoc on a culture and on politicians it does not like. Their theories often are correct but flawed because of timing. Such comments usually arise only when politicians must defend themselves against something they should not have been doing in the first place.

Nevertheless, the reality is that the mass media in this country is an enormous enterprise involving billions of dollars, employing millions of people, and affecting every person in the United States today and most of the rest of the world, too.

Indeed, Marshall McLuhan is correct when he speaks of our tribal world village. I remember vividly walking down an unpaved street in one of the slums of Santo Domingo, Dominican Republic, several years ago and seeing inside one shanty a color television blaring while semi-naked children played nearby on the dirt floor of their home. We are approaching the day when we can paraphrase the poet, "Breathes there a soul who never has said, 'What's on television tonight?'"

We cannot escape the mass media. We cannot evade the reality. We cannot turn back the clock 50 years. The media permeates our culture in such a way that we cannot accomplish anything without taking the mass media into account.

Thus, it is appropriate when we consider the environment and what we Christians can and should do about the destruction of God's earth that we include a discussion about "How to Deal with the Media on Ecological Issues."

A Media Bias Against Religion?

We face two major problems when we discuss this subject.

First, the mass media—no matter how marvelous it is—has some inherent weaknesses. One of those is its failure to come to grips with religious faith and morality.

Defenses go up when one says the media is biased against religion, yet the evidence is overwhelming. Study after study shows that members of the media—the movers and shakers, not the elevator operators and the classified ad salespersons in media buildings—tend to be somewhere between areligious and anti-religious in their personal perspective. In simple English: Editors and reporters attending church regularly are few and far between. Most studies indicate only about six percent of the news media is in church or synagogue on a regular basis. My personal experience in the media validates those figures.

But this personal reality is not nearly as important as is the attitude many in the media hold that religion simply does not belong in the public arena. To many, religion is a private subject—one that is best left unreported. I have known too many fine journalists who would argue that religion is not a fit subject for a newspaper. During the late 1970s and through much of the 1980s, I held every elective office in the national professional society of religion editors. I, along with my colleagues, was pleased that during that period of time the number of newspapers hiring full-time religion editors or writers grew dramatically. This was very, very good.

Yet, when we stood back and observed ourselves in context, we quickly realized that American newspapers during the 1980s went crazy hiring business, politics, and sports reporters, not religion reporters. Religion was way down on the list of priorities. Business reporting by far was the specialty reporting that swept the decade. Throughout the 1980s, newspapers around the nation thought nothing of expanding their business staffs by quantum leaps. As the decade ended, one still could count on one hand the number of newspapers in this country with more than one person assigned to cover religion. On far too many newspapers today, religion still is relegated to the least-favored beat.

And where are television's religion reporters? During the 1980s, Religion Newswriters Association debated at length whether to open its ranks to television reporters. While the debate raged, many of us kept asking when the number of religion reporters on television would be larger than what can assemble in a phone booth.

Like other American business enterprises, the media puts its resources where its heart is, and that is not in religion.

This bias shows itself in lack of attention to things religious unless some television preacher gets caught with his zipper down or when something equally important occurs.

A Late Jump on the Bandwagon

The second major problem we face involves something we may not want to hear. We are Johnnies-come-lately to the issues involving the environment. Concern with the environment began to take hold in this country in the 1960s. Except for a few Southern Baptists who climbed aboard the bandwagon but soon got off, our track record as a denomination on this issue is not good. One can't say it is bad. It just is not there. It is mostly nonexistent. We have done little in regard to preaching and proclaiming the message of God's love for all of His creation, including the earth.

Our focus is on saving souls, as well it should be. But I like what Roy Edgemon of the Baptist Sunday School Board said to me recently: "We are to care for the earth until Jesus comes." Discipling new Christians about biblical teachings on all things, including the importance of caring for God's creation, needs to be a major priority, too.

Thus, as we work to remind others that the Bible is clear in its command to care for the earth, we are subject to the charge of being involved with "old news." Our voices were not the first raised, and today many with whom we do not agree clamor on the public stage on this issue. The media, in case you have not noticed, is filled with stories and information about the environment.

So how do we deal with the media on ecological issues?

First, we should not back away from the issue just because we may be called Johnny-come-latelies. And besides, we really do bring a fresh perspective, a newsworthy angle, to the issue. Much of the environmental movement today lacks a solid Christian theological foundation. Seldom do people present earth care as a mandate from God, the creator and sustainer of all life. Instead, too often the concern seems to focus on love of creation in and of itself.

To make news and to deal with the media on this issue, we must speak up about the environment. We cannot fault the media for failing to report a story that does not exist. So, let's make it something that does exist. Rather than fighting over whether or how we came to be so far behind on this issue, our best approach is to admit our tardiness and get on with the task of spreading our message.

Figuring out ways to make news about our interest in the environment is important. Seminars represent a good starting place. We also should look for ways to articulate our concern about God's world and our stewardship of it. We should ask ourselves some important questions: When was the last time WE preached on the subject of the environment? When are WE going to put a sermon on the environment on our schedules?

Also, consider writing on this issue in columns in your church's newsletter. You can write about what your church can do or is doing regarding recycling. You can prompt some serious thought about stewardship being more than bringing the tithe into the storehouse. A good column would be one that provides your people with leadership regarding Earth Day.

Second, lead your church to take the initiative regarding issues pertaining to the environment. Does your church recycle its own garbage? When was the last time you offered at your church a seminar on recycling in the home or on a theology of ecology? Plan a special event on the environment, and invite your local media to come and cover it.

You might want to think about ways you could piggyback on Earth Day activities. Obviously some of what occurs surrounding Earth Day lacks a Christian perspective and focus. Nevertheless, Earth Day presents us with an interesting challenge in the media. Can we not capitalize on all the hoopla to try and get across our message that "The earth is the Lord's, and the fulness thereof; the world, and they that dwell therein" (Ps. 24:1, KJV)?

Do not misread me as endorsing Earth Day. I am raising some crucial questions about this colossal media event. In times past, Christians have reacted in different ways to major events in their culture. One reaction has been to retreat; another has been to baptize. Christmas trees, for instance, started out not as Christian symbols but as a pagan holiday decorations. European Christians eventually adopted the decoration but gave it new meaning with the star on top as a reminder of the Star of Bethlehem and the green fir tree as a reminder of the living message of Christmas. Rather than retreat from Earth Day because of its non-Christian underpinnings, Christians could adopt the good things in it and insert into it the foundational message of concern for the environment—that God is the author of creation.

Third, as we ponder ways to focus attention on the Christian's responsibility toward the environment, let us not hide our candles under bushels. Pat Pattillo, president of the Religious Public Relations Association, the national professional society, said in a recent article, "One of my favorite short definitions of PR is: Do good, then get the credit for it. There is nothing wrong with wanting to share the good news about what we are doing with others."[5]

Dealing with News Media Members

Here are a few tips on dealing specifically with members of the news media:

1. Remember that the media are plural. Marshall McLuhan did a wonderful job helping us understand the total picture of the change in human communications worldwide. Theories, however, represent only helpful background information when people try to make an impact on the media. Individuals who work in the various news operations in this country don't like to be grouped and labeled. Reporters and editors are defensive about being thought of as part of some great monolith.

Remember that the mass media is composed of individual components who often compete strenuously against one another. Houston federal judge Woodrow Seals, a leading United Methodist layman, once told me he believes the mass media is the last bastion of truly unregulated, uncontrolled free enterprise in this country. Many outlets make up the news media—TV, radio, newspapers, magazines. Each has its own unique ownership, its own philosophy, its own way of doing business. The quickest way to fail in trying to deal with the media is to see all members of the media as working lock-step.

2. Never forget that members of the news media are people, too. It is easy to stereotype any group, and members of the media are no exception. I have known many liberal, young, Yuppie, Eastern, rebellious types in the media who have given it its image. But I've also known many conservative, traditionalist types who would not join a rebellion even if their mother was leading it. When I worked in the *Houston Chronicle* city room, nearby were Chase Untermeyer, the consummate Republican and later an assistant to President George Bush, and Elmer Bertlesen, who was an Archie Bunker personified. No one would dare call either anything but conservative.

3. Tailor your approach to your individual situation. First, learn who the members of the media are in your hometown. Think widely. Just because you have always subscribed to one paper, do not forget the other. Read bylines. Read stories about the newspaper itself. Read the mast on the editorial page. Learn names.

Then meet the individuals. Reporters need sources. Make appointments, but keep them *brief.* And when you talk to employees of the media, don't offend. I'll never forget Dean Baxter, a Mormon, who wanted so much to influence me and couldn't help bungling his approaches. Dean was so busy trying to convert me to Mormonism and to persuade me to write from his perspective on Mormonism that I finally asked God to help me deal with this individual before I lost my temper with him. And don't forget, most reporters would rather tell a person they perceive as being out of line to get lost than to pray for direction in working with him or her.

Nevertheless, remember these ground rules:

1. Be persistent. If your first idea doesn't fly, don't give up.

Keep on trying, but be polite. When I was religion editor of the *Houston Chronicle*, I had an 18-inch-high stack of story ideas from readers. The longer I worked at that newspaper, the higher that stack grew. Each week I culled through my stack for pertinent ideas. I told people, "Please don't be offended if I don't use what you suggest. If I don't pick up on it, it's probably because of what was happening news-wise that week more than because of the merits of your story." I advised them to keep submitting suggestions, because eventually one of their ideas would surface.

2. Don't be afraid to repeat your message. Advertisers know that repetition eventually pays off. A good advertising salesperson will tell you that one ad is a shot in the dark but that a consistent, well-planned ad campaign reaps results.

3. Be articulate, especially about why Christians are or should be involved in environmental issues. When a member of the news media asks you to comment, be ready. Do your homework. Learn the skills of being interviewed. Practice effective communication.

4. Hang in there. We Christians have a responsibility to care for our environment. We do not have to apologize for that responsibility. We must do the work God has asked us to do. We must get the message out that "The earth is the Lord's, and the fulness thereof; the world, and they that dwell therein" (Ps. 24:1, KJV).

May God bless your efforts.

Notes

1. Marshall McLuhan and Quentin Fiore, *The Medium is the Massage* (New York: Bantam, 1967), 162.

2. Ronald T. Farrar, *Mass Communication: An Introduction to the Field* (New York: West, 1988), 241.

3. Ibid., 257

4. McLuhan, 2.

5. Wesley M. (Pat) Pattillo, "Staying A Jump Ahead of Trouble," *ECOlines,* Winter, 1991.

13

How a Local Church Can Begin a Recycling Program
Lamar E. Cooper, Sr.

Recycling is one way in which every individual, church, business, and community can do something positive to protect and to preserve the earth's environment. It also is a way to demonstrate Christian stewardship of the earth's resources.

Recycling is any organized system for collecting, reprocessing, and reusing materials once considered garbage. Every individual in America generates four to five pounds of garbage daily, more than 1,500 pounds annually, and as much as 90,000 pounds over a lifetime.[1] Our nation has run out of places to dispose of the garbage generated by its 250 million inhabitants.

As Diane MacEachern points out in her book, *Save Our Planet*, "Each year Americans throw away 18 billion disposable diapers, 1.7 billion disposable pens, 2 billion razors and blades, and 220 million tires. Enough aluminum is discarded to rebuild the entire U.S. commercial airline fleet every three months."[2] What happens to all of these items which are disposed of as a matter of mere convenience? Eighty percent of our nation's solid waste is being dumped and buried in the 6,000 landfills still in operation.[3] The other 20 percent will be considered a little later in this chapter.

From 1978 to 1988, nearly 70 percent (14,000) of the nation's 20,000 landfills closed because they were full. By 1993 an additional 2,000 will close.[4] We are running out of places to bury our garbage.

Landfills are not the answer to our garbage problem. They contaminate groundwater and create methane and other gases harmful to the atmosphere, humans, animals, and plants. They are not hotbeds of composting, as many people have thought. Little of the garbage buried during the last 20 years has decomposed. William Rathje, archeologist turned garbologist, has been excavating landfills created in the 1950s as part of an environmental project at the University of Arizona. His findings explode the myth that garbage, including food and yard waste, decomposes rapidly. Twenty-year-old newspapers still were readable. In another dig he excavated, a four-year-old landfill yielded hot dogs that were still intact and heads of almost passable lettuce.[5]

So far, we have mentioned only municipal waste. Industrial waste and toxic pollutants compound the solid waste problem even more. U.S. industry adds another 350 million tons of garbage annually to the waste disposal problem.[6] Hazardous waste is being produced at a rate of 700,000 tons per day and 250 million tons per year, coming primarily from manufacturing, using, and disposing of as many as 80,000 chemicals. Also, Americans use 270 million pounds of pesticides each year on lawns, gardens, and parks.[7]

These statistics represent no more than the tip of the iceberg of our garbage and solid waste problems. Such facts raise an appropriate question. Can we, as individuals, really do anything that will make a difference in our world for present and future generations? The answer is a resounding YES! We can become educated and involved in helping to address the industrial waste and toxic pollutant problem. We can become personally involved in our own homes, businesses, churches, and communities by reducing municipal waste.

Recycling is a viable alternative to burying garbage that immediately can reduce disposable waste by 60 to 80 percent. Seattle, Washington, has one of the best recycling programs for municipal waste in the nation. Seattle turned to recycling in 1986 when its landfills were full. Seattle neared its goal of reducing solid waste by 40 percent through recycling by the end of 1991. The ultimate goal of Seattle's citizens is to reduce solid waste by 60 percent by 1998.[8]

The Biblical Mandate

If we are to be salt and light, we no longer can ignore our responsibility for our world. This is an issue we must face during this decade. We don't have to choose between the gospel and the environment. We can be involved in both preaching the gospel and in being good environmental stewards. It is not the gospel or the environment; it is not evangelism or ethics; the issue is both.

Aside from the obvious need, when we recycle, we also fulfill a mandate God gave the human family. This mandate has four aspects to consider.

1. Humans are stewards of the planet, not owners. According to Genesis 2:15, RSV God gave humans a work assignment which included tilling and keeping the earth. The assignment to till (*abadh*, Hebrew) literally means *to work* or *to serve* the ground. It implies responsible use of the earth's resources. The word *abadh* is a verb form meaning *to serve* or *to work.* The very word *abadh* bears subtle but important witness to the fact that humans occupy the role of servants regarding the earth and its resources. "The earth is the Lord's . . ." (Ps. 24:1), His possession, and we are stewards who are to serve Him. One important way we serve God is by being responsible servants *(abadh)* of the earth and its resources.

The assignment to keep the earth is equally significant. The word *to keep* (*shamar*, Hebrew) literally means *to guard* and *to protect* something. Genesis 1:1 says, "God created" (*bara'*, a Hebrew term used only in reference to God.) Only God "creates" the heavens and the earth. God took the nothingness of nonexistent matter and from it formed all that exists. The universe belongs to Him by His divine creative right. He also created human beings to inhabit the earth and gave work which was to include guarding and protecting (*shamar*) from harm all the rest of His creative handiwork.

As stewards, our primary responsibility is faithfulness to these two God-assigned tasks which mandate that we be good stewards of all creation, especially His world. Our failure in both of these assignments has created a global crisis threatening the health and well-being of the earth and its inhabitants. Recycling is one positive way to return to the God-given role of responsible stewardship of the earth, which belongs to God.

2. Stewards have vested authority. Since we are not owners, the only authority we have is the authority God, who owns all things, gives us. Genesis 1:26 says God gave humans dominion over the heavens and the earth. The word *dominion* (*radah*, Hebrew) means *to rule* or *to dominate.* But this rule assigned to the human family is not an absolute rule. We are not free to do as we please with the world God gave us to rule. Genesis 1 presents Yahweh as the Creator-King of the universe.[9] The role assigned to human beings is one of vested authority. This means we are stewards, not owners, and we have no rights of our own which allow us to use the earth without regard for God, others, and ourselves. We are, therefore, responsible for prudent use of the planet and beyond, including all the visible and invisible universe.

3. Stewards are accountable. The next significant insight is that, as stewards, we will be held accountable before God for our stewardship of planet earth. Will it be poor or good stewardship? As stewards, humans are accountable to God, the owner, for whether we prudently use or wantonly abuse His creation.

Jesus' parable of the talents presents illustrative insight into this matter of our stewardship responsibility (Matt. 25:14-30; 1 Cor. 3:11-15; 2 Cor. 5:9-10). Judgment is a topic we mistakenly reserve in our minds for evildoers. But the Bible teaches that the people of God also are to be held accountable as stewards for time, possessions, and even life. Not only are we responsible to God, but we also have a responsibility to one another in the present generation and to future generations for how we use God's resources.

4. Stewards receive grace. Such an assignment of good stewardship of our world, ourselves, and others is overwhelming. The fact that we, evangelical Christians, have neglected our role as good

environmental stewards for so long increases the weight of our responsibility. We have allowed other voices, many of them non-Christian, to give the call to responsibility on environmental issues. The discomfort of the present failures and the prospect of future devastation finally has arrested our attention, begun to reshape our thinking, and finally called us to see our true role as stewards, not owners, nor users, nor consumers, nor exploiters of planet earth and the universe beyond.

Out of His grace, God sent His Son to redeem the world [*kosmos* in Greek, literally "the created order" (John 3:16)], and to remove the curse that sin brought to humanity and the environment (Gen. 3:14ff.; Rom. 8:22; Gal. 3:13; Rev. 22:1-3). Thus, it is only by the grace which God Himself offers that we are enabled to be good stewards of His world.

Given these four aspects of our stewardship, (1) it is God's world, (2) as stewards we have vested authority, (3) stewards are accountable to God, (4) stewards receive grace for their assignment, it becomes clear that we have a biblical mandate to be responsible inhabitants of our planet. We must consider all we have and how we will use it in light of how it will bring glory to God, the owner, and cause benefit to our neighbor. This is our assignment from our Creator-King.

Seven Serious Situations

Recycling is part of our responsibility to God, as Scripture outlines. On a more practical level, however, recycling has become a matter of life and death and of survival for the entire human family. The needs mentioned in the introduction to this chapter have given way to a serious global crisis. Elkington, Hailes, and Makower in *The Green Consumer* identify seven serious environmental problems, each one of which can be helped through recycling.[10]

1. Acid Rain. Sulfur dioxide is a gas which, when released into the atmosphere, creates acid rain. The two largest sources of sulfur dioxide released into our atmosphere are: (1)utilities burning coal and natural gas, and (2)fossil fuel engines in cars and trucks. Acid rain kills fish, wildlife, and plant life and contaminates groundwater. Utilities heat and light our homes and provide power for business and industry. Whenever we conserve energy, we also reduce sulfur dioxide which causes acid rain.

Recycling aluminum cans saves energy. Each recycled aluminum can saves 95 percent of the energy consumed in production. Thus, every time you recycle one aluminum can, you cut sulfur dioxide pollutants by 95 percent of what would have been generated by the production of one new aluminum can. Twenty cans may be recycled with the same amount of energy required to make one can from new material.[11] Recycling reduces air pollutants and is one way we can help alleviate the acid rain problem in our world.

2. Global Warming. The year 1990 was the warmest on record to date since people have kept weather statistics. As global warming continues, scientists foresee major changes in climate, agriculture, sea levels, and other problems. The greenhouse effect is exacerbated by the use of fossil fuels which produce carbon dioxide, chloroflurocarbons (called CFC's) used as coolants, methane, and other gases from landfills, and nitrous oxide from chemical fertilizers.[12] Recycling can reduce energy consumption, as already noted, eliminate the need for more landfills, reduce CFC's, and help alleviate the global warmup exacerbated by the carbon dioxide buildup in the atmosphere.

3. Ozone depletion. The ozone layer is a protective shield from harmful solar and celestial radiation for all life on planet earth. As a result of this depletion in the ozone layer, the incidence of sunburn and resultant skin cancer is on the rise. Australia is the continent nearest to Antarctica where experts have discovered holes in the ozone layer. Shifting patches of ozone-depleted atmosphere over Australia occasionally have pushed ultraviolet radiation 20 percent above normal. News and weather reports in Australia now include ultraviolet readings and warnings to stay inside during high-level radiation. Australia already leads the world in the incidence of skin cancer.[13] [Editor's note: As this book goes to press, new concerns have arisen about reported ozone holes over the United States and Western Europe.]

Chloroflurocarbons (CFC's) represent the culprit in ozone depletion. They are used in aerosol cans, units using coolants, fire extinguishers, and Styrofoam. When burned in incinerators, Styrofoam pollutes the atmosphere with CFC's.[14] By recycling this and other plastics, we can reduce harmful emissions. People also are attempting to begin to recycle coolants from air conditioners and refrigeration units rather than to bleed them into the atmosphere. All efforts in these areas will help alleviate future damage to the ozone layer.

4. Air Pollution. The Environmental Protection Agency (EPA) has identified 320 toxic pollutants in the air we breathe. Since hydrocarbons from fossil fuels and nitrous oxides represent the major source of pollution, we help reduce air pollution when we save energy by recycling.[15] Also, we must be diligent to insist that industrial pollutants be monitored and regulated. Only seven of the 320 toxic pollutants currently are regulated by the EPA.

5. Depletion of rain forests. Tropical forests are being destroyed at a rate of 27 million acres annually. This affects our atmosphere in two basic ways. First, the burning uses oxygen and creates more carbon dioxide for the already overburdened atmosphere. Second, trees, like other plants, breathe carbon dioxide and give off oxygen.[16] Fewer trees means less carbon dioxide consumed and less oxygen produced. Recycling wood and wood byproducts, such as paper, can help with this problem.

6. Garbage. The problems created by failure to recycle garbage involve everything we already have discussed. Garbage is a major factor in the continued pollution of air, water, and ground. Failure to recycle our trash makes us larger energy consumers and creates more hazardous waste and pollutants for our environment.[17]

7. Water. Landfills and dumping toxic waste represent just two of the ways we continue to pollute the waters of our planet.[18] Water pollution certainly is a growing global problem which we can help alleviate through recycling.

If we choose to ignore these problems or to disregard the seriousness of their impact, we will abandon our responsibility as good stewards of our planet and its resources. Not only we but also our children, grandchildren, and great-grandchildren will feel this accountability.

How to Begin Recycling

Since we have established the need for recycling by reviewing the need, our biblical responsibility, and the current crises, the next issue to consider is a practical one. How can an individual, church, community, business, or others interested in an effective recycling program begin one?

1. Effective recycling begins with precycling. Consider the amount of garbage to be generated before buying a product. We no longer can afford to be consumers who give no thought to the by-products of our actions. Buy products made from recycled material. Look for the recycling logo on packaging. This indicates that the packaging either has been or can be recycled. Purchase items that are packed in recycled packaging. Many major corporations finally have grasped the seriousness of the problem and are adopting the use of recycled materials in their products. Reject product brands that are overpackaged or that refuse to use recycled or recyclable packaging. Avoid plastics whenever possible.

2. Reduce disposable garbage by reusing items at home and work. Use glasses and mugs instead of paper or Styrofoam cups, rags instead of paper towels, cloth diapers instead of plastic disposables, cloth instead of paper napkins, and so forth. The use of disposable items, in most cases, is a matter of convenience and not one of necessity. The use of such items greatly contributes to the garbage glut with which our and future generations must cope. We must not sacrifice health and well-being for convenience.

3. Separate recyclables into categories. Secure a container for each category: clear glass, colored glass, aluminum, tin/steel cans, plastics, motor oil, and compostable garbage.

Start a compost pile outdoors as a means of reusing waste food.

Also, a compost pile can include grass clippings and leaves, along with biodegradable foodstuffs.

4. Place separated items in a recycling bin. Many communities are beginning some form of recycling program from curbside to community containers. Some supermarkets and other businesses have placed recycling bins on their property to encourage recycling. As the garbage glut increases, more of these will become available.

Rural homes and communities present the greatest challenge because recycling bins are not as available in these areas. Recycled items must be taken to the nearest village or urban collection center.

5. Begin a recycling program in your church or community. People can obtain recycling bins, often at no charge, and can place them in any community or rural area. Being a good steward of the planet involves being an informed steward. Obtain from your state recycling coordinator information on places where recycling collection facilities are situated. Every state in the nation has a recycling coordinator. *The Recycler's Handbook* is an excellent resource. It contains a list of recycling agencies by state, as well as state and national recycling associations.[19] Also, *Coming Full Circle*, a report published by the Environmental Defense Fund, contains the name, address, and telephone number of the recycling coordinator in each state, recycling industry associations, and state recycling hot line 800 telephone numbers.[20]

What Can Be Recycled?

Most people are aware of the big three recycling items: paper, aluminum cans, and glass. Many other items also can be recycled, as well as items in these three categories, that may not normally occur to most people. The largest percentage of solid waste in our garbage is paper (42.1 percent).[21] This involves newsprint, magazines, cardboard boxes, packaging, office papers, and so forth. The next largest item in the garbage can is food and yard waste, such as leaves and grass clippings (23.4 percent). Glass containers account for the third largest item (9.4 percent), followed closely by metals in fourth place (9.2 percent). Plastics account for the fifth largest item (6.5 percent), and other miscellaneous items account for 9.4 percent of all solid waste.

Currently, we recycle only about 10 percent of our solid waste. Of the remaining garbage, 80 percent is buried in landfills, and 10 percent is incinerated.[22] We must become much more conscious about what can be recycled and must commit ourselves to take the extra time and effort to rescue these items from our nation's garbage cans.

The following is a list of items that may not have occurred to you as possible items for recycling:

Batteries—These include auto and household batteries (buy rechargeable ones).

Junk mail—Stopping junk mail can reduce your waste paper significantly.[23]

Tires—We throw away from 220 to 250 million tires per year.[24]

Appliances/Furniture—Recycle unwanted items or sell them.

Motor Oil—If you use an oil-change center, ask if they recycle the oil.

Styrofoam—Burning this material creates CFC's.

Plastics—Bags and shrink wraps are included.

Steel—Toys, old cars, and swings are examples.

Metals—Copper, brass, and stainless steel are among the most-used metals.

Clothes—If they are usable, give them to distributors. If they are not, recycle them.

Freon—This and other CFC refrigerants can be recycled. If you have your home or car air conditioner serviced, ask service people if they recycle this refrigerant to stop ozone depletion.

Food—Create compost by using waste food and scraps to make fresh soil.

People can set up a composting area in the yard of a home, business, or church. Compost is a combination of grass clippings, leaves, and foodstuffs placed in a composting bin or pile. This process allows living organisms to feed on the organic material and to turn it into a rich crumbly soil called humus. Information on how to compost is readily available at most garden shops or hardware stores.

Recycling Resources

Books

The Recycler's Handbook by The Earth Works Group. Berkeley, CA: Earthworks, 1990.

50 Simple Things You Can Do to Save the Earth by The Earth Works Group. Berkeley, CA: Earthworks, 1989.

50 Simple Things Kids Can Do to Save the Earth by The Earth Works Group. New York: Andrews and McMeel, 1990.

The Green Consumer by John Elkington, Julia Hailes, and Joel Makower. New York: Penguin Books, 1990.

Save Our Planet by Diane MacEachern. New York: Dell, 1990.

War on Waste by Louis Blumberg and Robert Gottlieb. Washington, DC: Island, 1989.

Report

Coming Full Circle: Successful Recycling Today. A comprehensive report on beginning and maintaining community recycling programs. Available from the Environmental Defense Fund, 257 Park Avenue, 5, New York, NY 10010 (cost, $20).

Magazines

Garbage: The Practical Journal for the Environment. P. 0. Box 56519, Boulder, CO 80322-6579 ($21 per year).

World Watch. World Watch Institute, 1776 Massachusetts Avenue, NW, Washington, DC 20036 ($15 per year).

Pamphlets

"The Bible Speaks on Ecology." The Christian Life Commission, 901 Commerce Street, Suite 550, Nashville, TN 37203-3696 (17 cents each).

"Recycling: Treasure in Our Trash." Waste Recyclers Council, National Solid Wastes Management Association, 1730 Rhode Island Avenue, NW, Washington, DC 20036 (single copies free upon request).

Notes

1. *The Recycler's Handbook*, 13.
2. *Save Our Planet*, 9.
3. Ibid.
4. *The Recycler's Handbook*, 13.
5. "Garbologist Trashes Lab Theories," *USA Today*, 4/20/90, 11E.
6. "Waste not, Why not?" *American Way*, 4/15/90, 48.
7. *Save Our Planet*, 5-6.
8. *American Way*, 52.
9. Geerhardus Vos, *Biblical Theology*, (Grand Rapids: Eerdmans, 1971), 398; Charles A. Briggs, *Messianic Prophecy* (New York: Scribners, 1886), 70.
10. *The Green Consumer*, 12-58.
11. *The Recycler's Handbook*, 32.
12. *The Green Consumer*, 14-17.
13. See *World Watch* (September-October, 1990), 6.
14. *The Green Consumer*, 17-20.
15. Ibid., 20-22.
16. Ibid., 22-26.
17. Ibid., 26-28
18. Ibid., 28-31.
19. *The Recycler's Handbook*, 117-26.
20. *Coming Full Circle*, 147-156.
21. "Recycling: Treasure in Our Trash," (Washington, DC: National Solid Wastes Management Association, 1988), 2.
22. *The Green Consumer*, 26.
23. *50 Simple Things You Can Do to Save the Earth*, 20.
24. *The Recycler's Handbook*, 96-97.